TEMPLES
of
DELIGHT

Stowe Landscape Gardens

OVERLEAF
Looking across the Eleven-Acre Lake towards
Vanbrugh's Rotunda. The Eleven-Acre Lake formed
part of Bridgeman's original layout of the 1720s and is
the western extension of the stretch of water that
fills the whole shallow valley along the south end of the garden.

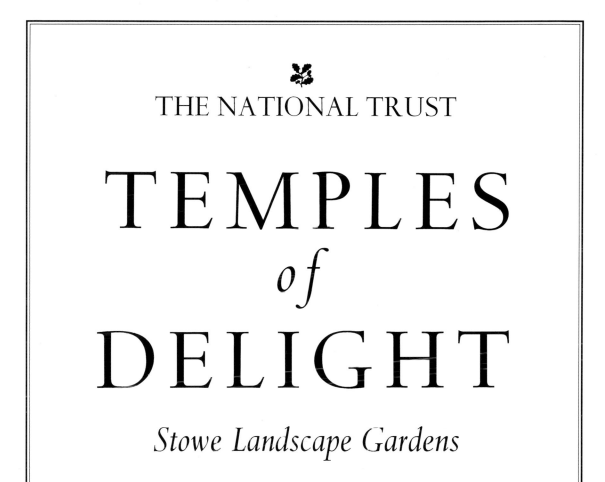

THE NATIONAL TRUST

TEMPLES

of

DELIGHT

Stowe Landscape Gardens

JOHN MARTIN ROBINSON

Colour photography by

JERRY HARPUR

THE NATIONAL TRUST · GEORGE PHILIP

Stowe Landscape Gardens Appeal

Contributions to the appeal may be sent to the Special
Appeals Manager (Stowe), The National Trust,
36 Queen Anne's Gate, London SW1H 9AS.

Published by George Philip Limited,
59 Grosvenor Street, London W1X 9DA,
in association with
The National Trust, 36 Queen Anne's Gate, London SW1H 9AS

Text © John Martin Robinson 1990
Jerry Harpur photography © The National Trust 1990

British Library Cataloguing in Publication Data
Robinson, John Martin
Temples of delight: Stowe Landscape Gardens,
Buckinghamshire.
1. England. Landscape gardens, history
I. Title   II. Harpur, Jerry   III. National Trust
712.60942

ISBN 0—540—01217—3

Book design by Simon Bell

Printed in Hong Kong

Phototypeset by Keyspools Limited,
Golborne, Lancs

CONTENTS

ACKNOWLEDGMENTS

FIRST AND FOREMOST, anybody who writes about Stowe owes a great debt of gratitude to George Clarke, Chairman of the Stowe Advisory Committee, whose detailed researches into the history of the development of the Stowe landscape make up the major source of information about the place. In addition, where this book is concerned, George Clarke has provided much additional help and information and has patiently read and corrected the manuscript. Mr M. J. Bevington, the Head of Classics and archivist at Stowe School, has also provided considerable assistance.

Richard Wheeler, the National Trust's managing agent, Rosemary Jury, the Trust's Administrator at Stowe, Frank Thomson, the Head Gardener, and Peter Inskip, the architect, have all been of great assistance. Gervase Jackson-Stops, the Historic Buildings Representative for Stowe, has provided much useful information as well as reading and commenting on my manuscript. Sukie Hemming, on behalf of the Stowe Landscape Gardens Appeal, commissioned the very beautiful new photography by Jerry Harpur, Diana Lanham, the Trust's Photographic Librarian, also anguished over the photography, and Samantha Wyndham has magnificently collected the pictures and patiently tracked down elusive prints and drawings. Margaret Willes, the National Trust Publisher, as always, has provided good-humoured support. Lydia Greeves at George Philip painstakingly edited the text, and Margaret Lancaster prepared the typescript.

John Martin Robinson
Beckside House, Barbon
April 1990

STOWE AND THE NATIONAL TRUST

OVERLEAF
A feature of the layout at
Stowe is the series of
contrived vistas towards
carefully sited
monuments, as in this
view along the Octagon
Lake towards the
Palladian Bridge.

WHEN THE FOUNDERS of the school bought Stowe in 1922, they can have had little idea of what they were taking on, for at the time landscape gardening, like other aspects of eighteenth-century culture, was almost totally unappreciated. In the 1918 edition of Methuen's *Little Guide* to Buckinghamshire, for instance, Stowe was dismissed as 'a melancholy relic of eighteenth-century taste', whose grounds were 'filled with all sorts of pseudo-classical erections'.

Such a philistine attitude seems inconceivable today, but that in itself is a measure of the change in aesthetic opinion which has taken place during the last seventy years. From the start, however, there were always enlightened individuals who perceived the genius of the place. We realize now what a miracle it was that Clough Williams-Ellis should have been chosen as the school's first architect. A decade later Christopher Hussey, author of *The Picturesque*, began to foster a wider understanding of landscape gardens like Stowe.

These and other pioneers gradually brought about a change of attitude. After World War II, and with increasing momentum from the 1960s, the school authorities made strenuous efforts to repair the garden buildings and to rehabilitate the landscape. Alongside the restorers worked the historians, to make sure that the restoration was based on sound scholarship. Every item of building work, which was aided throughout by grants from the Historic Buildings Council (later English Heritage), was approved by its architects; and after the signing of the covenant with the National Trust in 1967, all the work on the landscape gardens was guided by the Trust's consultants. Six of the eighteenth-century avenues, collapsed or in terminal decay, were replaced, tree by tree. Over 20,000 young trees were planted in the park and woodlands. Repairs, major or minor, were carried out on no fewer than twenty-six of the garden buildings.

Few estates can claim to have done so much, but none has so much to do — and that is the core of the problem. Stowe has more than twice as many listed garden buildings as any other English garden, and as building costs began to soar in the 1980s it became less and less likely that the repair programme would ever catch up with dilapidation. The Stowe Gardens Buildings Trust was established as a charitable trust in 1986 in an attempt to attract more funds, enabling full repairs to be carried out to the drum and dome of the Temple of Ancient Virtue, but meanwhile the Corinthian Arch, the Temple of Concord and Victory, the Temple of Venus and other buildings were slipping into worse disrepair. It seemed that all we were achieving was to postpone Stowe's final disintegration.

Then, out of the blue, an anonymous benefactor came forward with an offer of £2 million towards repairs, on condition that the school handed ownership of the gardens and temples over to the National Trust. In July 1989, agreement was finally reached and Stowe, apart from the mansion and other school facilities, passed to the Trust.

A substantial sum is still needed to repair individual buildings, and for this the Trust has launched a special appeal of £1 million: royalties from the sale of this book will go towards that appeal. Subject to the appeal's success, the chronic shortage of funds for restoration should now be a thing of the past. A liberal grant of £4.5 million by the National Heritage Memorial Fund, the promise of continued aid from English Heritage, and the Landmark Trust's generous offer to take over the Corinthian Arch have put the financial base of Stowe's gardens and garden buildings on a sounder footing than it has been for two hundred years.

One of the Trust's first jobs is to make a detailed survey of the whole property: it is intended that this will be a model of its kind, fully integrating archaeological, documentary and visual evidence with the landscape survey, and setting the standard for similar surveys in the future. Another essential is to survey all the garden buildings so that a detailed repair programme can be made up to the year 2000 and beyond. In the first year work will continue on the Temple of Ancient Virtue and repairs are planned on the Grenville Column, the Seasons' Fountain and the Doric Arch.

Under the protection of the National Trust, Stowe can resume its place as one of the classic gardens of the Western World.

George Clarke
Dorchester
April 1990

INTRODUCTION

STOWE IS THE largest, grandest and most important landscape garden in England. Situated on a south-facing hillside in mild undulating country to the north of Buckingham, the garden covers approximately 400 acres, all enclosed in an irregular pentagonal framework of avenues and ha-has, with projecting bastions at the corners like a Hanoverian fortification. It is one mile across at its widest extent and about two-thirds of a mile from north to south, with the mansion itself in the centre of the north side.

The garden is only the nucleus of an even larger planned landscape. It is surrounded to the south, east and west by an outer fringe of conventional wooded English parkland, while to the north-east the vestigial remains of a formal forest layout with long rides and wedges of woodland extend as far as the Northamptonshire border. In addition, Stowe is approached from west and south by two straight and immensely grand avenues of oak, lime, beech and chestnut; the Oxford Avenue follows a Roman alignment from the Brackley road, while the Grand Avenue runs for one and a half miles from the suburban fringes of Buckingham to the Triumphal Arch, sixty feet high, which crowns the ridge a mile to the south of the house. The scale and grandeur of the whole gives to Stowe something of the air of a capital or seat of government and this is not coincidental: in the eighteenth century, Stowe was one of the half dozen principal seats of the Whig aristocracy, and its owners, the Temple-Grenvilles, were a dominant force in the political life of the country. Here policy was framed, governments made or broken, the Court kept under jealous surveillance, liberty defended and the expansion of the British Empire planned.

As well as being a major work of art, the Stowe landscape is a monument to the liberal political beliefs of the Whigs, those descendants of the group of noblemen, gentry and merchants whose opposition to the absolutist ambitions of the Stuart monarchy had culminated in the Glorious Revolution of 1688. They could claim as a result to have established constitutional monarchy and political freedom in England and saw themselves as the defenders of liberty. Throughout the eighteenth century, the proprietors of Stowe and their relations were steadfast, if independent, adherents of the Whig cause in politics. This political allegiance runs through the garden architecture like a leitmotif, with temples, inscriptions and monuments recalling the vicissitudes of politics in eighteenth-century Britain.

During that time three successive owners of the estate enlarged and remodelled the garden to make it the pre-eminent example of

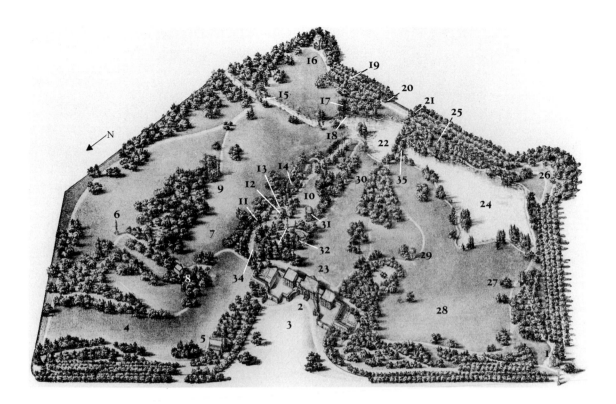

STOWE LANDSCAPE GARDENS

1 Boycott Pavilions
2 North Front
3 Statue of George I
4 Grecian Valley
5 Temple of Concord and Victory
6 Cobham Monument
7 Hawkwell Field
8 Queen's Temple
9 Gothic Temple
10 Elysian Fields
11 Seasons' Fountain
12 Cook Monument
13 Shell Bridge
14 Temple of British Worthies
15 Palladian Bridge
16 Temple of Friendship
17 Pebble Alcove
18 Congreve Monument
19 Bridgeman's Ha-ha
20 East Lake Pavilion
21 West Lake Pavilion
22 Octagon Lake
23 South Front
24 Eleven-Acre Lake
25 Hermitage
26 Temple of Venus
27 Queen Caroline's Monument
28 Home Park
29 Rotunda
30 Doric Arch
31 Temple of Ancient Virtue
32 St Mary's Church
33 Grenville Column
34 Grotto
35 Cascade

Wedgwood plaque of
Thomas Pitt, Lord
Camelford, a relation of
Earl Temple and an
amateur architect who
was responsible for the
Corinthian Arch, the
amended design for the
south front of the house,
and probably the
Doric Arch.

the English landscape movement, of which it can also claim to have been the chief pioneer. Many of the leading architects, landscape gardeners and sculptors of the age were employed to create the idealized classical landscape which exists today. Embellished with innumerable temples, columns, obelisks, arches, statues, urns and lakes, the Stowe landscape evokes the world of Ancient Rome which the new Augustan age of Georgian England confidently sought to outdo. Initially formal in design, Stowe pioneered the revolution towards the more naturalistic landscapes of grassy vistas, serpentine waters and informal tree-planting that 'Capability' Brown (head gardener at Stowe from 1741 to 1751) popularized throughout England, and indeed Europe.

The influence of Stowe has been immense and for three centuries its garden has been a mecca for curious visitors of all nationalities and all ranks, from royalty downwards. It has inspired copies across the world, from Russia to America. Outside St Petersburg, the Empress Catherine the Great created a new garden at Tsarskoe Selo which contains paraphrases of some of the Stowe buildings, while the architectural design of the Capitol in Washington, with the exception of the added dome, owes much to the south front of Stowe. In scale, influence and artistic originality, Stowe is to the *jardin anglais* what Versailles is to the formal baroque garden, and its progeny are as extensive.

During the course of the eighteenth century the Temple-Grenville family successively transformed Stowe from a small and circumscribed formal garden with terraces and geometrical ponds to a three-dimensional equivalent of the landscape paintings of Claude and Poussin or the poetry of Milton and Pope. The chief proponents were: Richard Temple, 1st Viscount Cobham; Richard, 2nd Earl Temple, and George, 1st Marquess of Buckingham. They employed many of the greatest names in English Georgian art: the architects Sir John Vanbrugh, James Gibbs, William Kent and Robert Adam; the gardeners Charles Bridgeman and 'Capability' Brown; the sculptors John Nost, Peter Scheemakers and John Michael Rysbrack. Nor was the roll-call of designers limited to native talent: Giacomo Leoni, Georges-François Blondel, Giovanni Battista Borra, Francesco Sleter and Vincenzo Valdrè added a Continental dimension, while Thomas Pitt, Lord Camelford (a nephew by marriage), and the owners themselves, notably Viscount Cobham and Earl Temple, played an important part in the garden's conception. Thus Stowe also represents the amateur design tradition which is such an interesting aspect of the Georgian age; gardening in particular in this period became a favourite relaxation of the aristocracy.

The Stowe garden was begun in the 1680s by Sir Richard Temple, 3rd Baronet, who rebuilt the Tudor house he had inherited and laid out a series of terraces and orchards on a south-facing slope, with its central axis aligned on the spire of Buckingham parish church three miles away. His son, Richard, later Viscount Cobham, enlarged and developed this layout from 1713 till his death in 1749, to create one of the most famous gardens in England. His initial work was still partly formal in that it comprised straight walks and avenues, clipped hedges, geometrical ponds and fountains. But this framework incorporated many departures from strict symmetry and areas of contrived naturalism, while the whole was opened up to the surrounding countryside by the consistent use of ha-has, then a novel device in England.

Lord Cobham's later work was progressively naturalistic and was continued by his nephew and successor, Earl Temple, who remodelled much of the garden, thinning the plantations, widening and naturalizing all the vistas and, not least, remodelling the façades

Looking across the park from the Corinthian Arch to the south front of the house. This view shows the vast scale of the Stowe layout.

of the house and many of the ornamental buildings to suit the new scale of their setting. The last touches were added towards the end of the eighteenth century by his nephew and heir, the Marquess of Buckingham. Thereafter, thanks to the increasingly straitened family finances, his successors, the Dukes of Buckingham, left the garden in its eighteenth-century state. As a result, it survived into the twentieth century unaffected by the swings of Victorian fashion, and remains today very largely in the condition which it had attained by the 1780s, though after World War I it ceased to be a private house and entered into another life as the seat of a new public school.

As it exists now, the Stowe garden comprises three main parts. The most impressive feature is the principal south axis, the main vista, which consists of a vast tapering sweep of lawn (covering the site of the original seventeenth-century terraces and orchards). This stretches down to a naturalized lake and is framed by artfully arranged plantations of forest trees, just like the flats in a stage set; beyond the lake, an amphitheatre of parkland is crowned by the Triumphal Arch, which also serves as the focus of the Grand Avenue from Buckingham on the other side of the hill. To the west of the central vista is the earliest extension of the garden, which was laid out by Viscount Cobham between 1713 and 1730 to the design of Charles Bridgeman, the royal gardener. But this is no longer in its original state, for it was remodelled and made more naturalistic in the 1740s and 1750s. Bridgeman's enclosing ha-ha and straight avenues still survive round the perimeter, as do one or two of the ornamental buildings, such as Kent's Temple of Venus and Vanbrugh's Rotunda. The Eleven-Acre Lake at the south end also remains, but the central area is now an irregularly shaped lawn with the Rotunda, once the focus of several straight paths, isolated on a gentle knoll. Thus the west garden is merely a palimpsest of Bridgeman's layout; the vanished hedges, statuary, straight gravel paths and moulded earthworks have to be imagined in the mind's eye.

To the east of the main vista, the third area of the garden survives largely in the form laid out by Viscount Cobham in the 1730s and 1740s. It is divided into three subsections: the Elysian Fields, Hawkwell Meadow and the Grecian Valley, each of which forms a classic self-contained landscape of its own.

The Elysian Fields fill a long narrow declivity parallel to the main vista. The banks of the serpentine stream following the valley are dotted with allegorical structures designed by William Kent and expressive of the political, philosophic, historical and literary concerns and allegiances of Lord Cobham and his circle, notably the Temple of Ancient Virtue and the Temple of British Worthies.

View from the Palladian Bridge at sunset.

OVERLEAF
The Corinthian Arch seen from the Octagon Lake. Designed by Lord Camelford in 1765, this triumphal arch is sixty feet high and the principal object on the great south vista from the house. The view up the park slopes is flanked by the Lake Pavilions.

Hawkwell Meadow is much larger in scale than the Elysian Fields and was conceived as a *ferme ornée**, with a central area given over to grazing animals or haymaking and surrounded by a carriage drive, with contrived views in and out, and a series of substantial garden buildings designed by James Gibbs. Of these, the gothic Temple of Liberty forms the visual climax to the political iconography of the Stowe landscape.

The third and latest of the subsections is the Grecian Valley in the north-east corner of the garden. This is a broadly 'painted' classical landscape with just a single temple gazing down an artificial vale defined by belts of trees planted in the grand and seemingly simple manner of 'Capability' Brown. As head gardener, Brown was partly responsible for its planting, and he was to popularize this kind of approach to landscaping once he had set up on his own account in the 1750s.

Thus the Stowe layout is illustrative of the three principal phases of English eighteenth-century landscape design, from the grandiose phase of Bridgeman's layout, through the allegorical classical scenery of Kent *et alia* to the grandly naturalistic vistas associated with 'Capability' Brown. In this, the Stowe landscape is unique. None of the other surviving English landscape gardens can display such a range. Castle Howard or Bramham (both in Yorkshire) illustrate the heroic phase on a comparably grand scale. Rousham (Oxfordshire) or Stourhead (Wiltshire) are consummate examples of contrived classical arcadia, while Bowood (Wiltshire), Harewood (Yorkshire) and many other parks survive in the fully-fledged English landscape manner on the noblest scale. But in no other place can the whole history of the landscape movement be traced in a single garden. Nor is the special interest of Stowe confined to that alone. It contains more temples than any other English eighteenth-century layout. Even today, 32 temples and associated buildings survive, many of them as big as houses. It was almost as if the family deliberately set out to create a three-dimensional pun on their own motto, *Templa quam dilecta* (How beautiful are thy temples).

Originally there were even more buildings, but as the scale of the garden developed so the buildings, as well as the trees, were thinned out. Despite this, many late Georgian visitors thought that there seemed to be too many of them. Prince Pückler-Muskau, for instance, a Polish adventurer who visited Stowe in the early nineteenth century, wrote in his journal: 'The grounds were laid out long ago, and though in many respects beautiful and remarkable for

The Pebble Alcove is adorned with Viscount Cobham's arms and the punning Temple family motto: *Templa quam dilecta* (How beautiful are thy temples).

* A working farm combining beauty with utility.

fine lofty trees, are so over-loaded with temples of all sorts, that the greatest possible improvement to the place would be the pulling down of ten or a dozen of them.' Lord Lyttelton, a cousin of the owners of Stowe, had already expressed a similar view as early as 1778: 'The huddling together of every species of building into a park or garden is ridiculous ... Fine woods are beautiful objects, and their beauty approaches nearer to magnificence as the mass of foliage becomes more visible; but to dot them with little white edifices infringes upon their greatness and destroys their due effect. Our climate is not fitted to the deities of Italy and Greece, and in a hard winter I feel for the shuddering divinities.' Such carping, however, rather missed the point. The architecture was at least as important as the planting in creating the effects which the Temple-Grenvilles and their designers were aiming at; to evoke a mood, to point a political allegory or stress a literary allusion.

The early landscape garden was designed to stimulate the mind of onlookers by means of emblematic devices, such as temples, inscriptions and statues, as well as by the scenery itself. Such gardens can be 'read' like works of literature. Though planned to look natural, the Augustan landscape was totally artificial. The aim was idealized nature, the creation of an arcadia, similar to the evocations of ancient Rome in seventeenth-century landscape painting or in classical literature.

Joseph Addison, the editor of *The Spectator* and one of the literary figures who helped to popularize the new landscape garden, described Virgil's *Georgics*, for instance, as 'a collection of the most delightful Landskips that can be made out of Fields and woods, Herds of cattle and Swarms of Bees'. To Lord Cobham and his contemporaries, the hay-making activity in Hawkwell Meadow, as framed in the portico of the Temple of Friendship, or the 'gadding heifers' in the home park as glimpsed from Vanbrugh's Rotunda would instantly have struck a particular literary chord and evoked the Golden Age.

The idealized landscape compositions at Stowe were intended not just to look pretty. They were dedicated to moods and the evocation of mythological scenes or the statement of political and moral principles; their content would have been instantly recognizable to contemporaries because of their similarity to the subjects depicted in Italian paintings and their derivation from literary sources. In his *Ichnographia Rustica* of 1718, Stephen Switzer, the writer and gardener, assembled an anthology of writings on landscape drawn from the works of Horace, Virgil, Milton and other writers. The *Ichnographia* had a considerable impact on contemporary garden design, much of which is redolent of poetic language. Such literary overtones are to

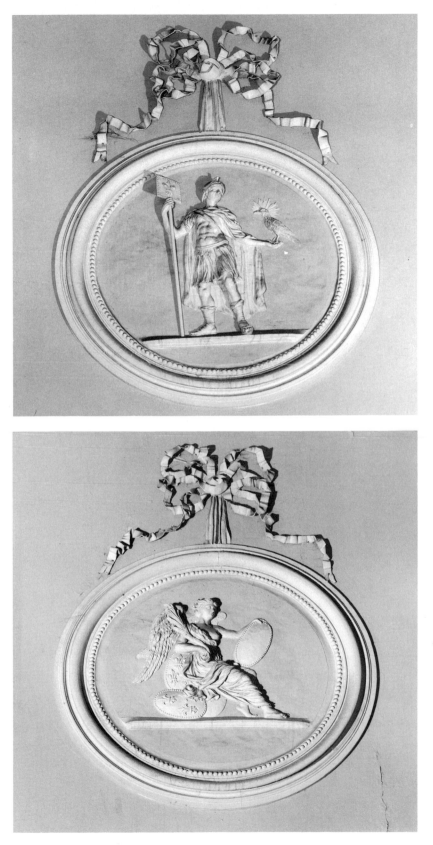

Plaques designed by Giovanni Battista Borra inside the Temple of Concord and Victory, depicting Britain's victories over France in the Seven Years' War.

OVERLEAF LEFT
The garden at Stowe contains many allusions to Lord Cobham's literary enthusiasms. William Congreve, the playwright, was a personal friend and this charming monument designed by William Kent was erected to him after his death.

OVERLEAF RIGHT
The Hermitage is a characteristic rustic exercise by Kent. The wreath in the pediment encloses a carving of Pan's pipes.

be found in nearly all Georgian gardens. But once again, Stowe is unique in the extent of its literary associations. Many of the leading writers and poets of the age were the close personal friends of its creator, Viscount Cobham, and their influence can still be appreciated. Monuments to Alexander Pope and William Congreve are among the garden ornaments. Busts of Shakespeare, Milton and Bacon adorn the Temple of British Worthies. The interiors of the Temple of Venus and the Hermitage were, originally, decorated with paintings from Spenser's *Faerie Queene*. The Lake Pavilions were likewise embellished with scenes from Guarini's sixteenth-century pastoral drama *Il Pastor Fido*. The Seasons Fountain bears an inscription from Thomson's *The Seasons*, and in the third (1744) edition of that popular 'nature' poem, Thomson added to the text of Autumn a lengthy verse description of 'the fair majestic paradise of Stowe' (lines 1037–1081). Not least, one of the temples designed by Gibbs is dedicated to Pastoral Poetry. The whole inspiration for the Elysian Fields was derived from Joseph Addison's famous essays in *The Spectator*. And Pope dedicated the first of his *Epistles* to Lord Cobham.

Many of the inscriptions (in Latin or English) which adorn the monuments, whether they are quotations from classical sources or were specially composed by members of the Stowe set, are of considerable literary merit. Rarely has the praise of famous men been more resonantly expressed than in the Temple of British Worthies at Stowe. There we can read of Milton, 'whose sublime and unbounded genius equall'd a subject that carried him beyond the limits of the world'; and of Drake, 'who, through many perils, was the first of Britons that ventured to sail round the globe; and carried into unknown seas and nations the knowledge and glory of the English name'. So rich and full, indeed, is Stowe in its associations and atmosphere that it might almost have been 'consciously prepared and soaked in history with the subsequent education of posterity in view'. In the words of Clough Williams-Ellis, the architect who adapted the place for its new use as a public school in the 1920s: 'It is to be doubted, indeed, whether any other of all the great houses in England has such associations for us, either directly through its past owners and their connexions, through its long list of royal and distinguished visitors, or indirectly through the temples and monuments that embellish the place, which, themselves designed by great architects, are for the most part dedicated to Greek philosophers or great Englishmen. All the honourable professions, the arts and virtues are represented, being celebrated both in dedicated monuments and by inscriptions.'

I

THE DYNASTY

To build, to plant, whatever you intend,
To rear the column, or the arch to bend,
To swell the terrace, or to sink the grot,
In all, let nature never be forgot.
Consult the genius of the place in all,
That tells the waters or to rise, or fall,

Or helps the ambitious hill the heavens to scale,
Or scoops in circling theatres the vale,
Calls in the country, catches opening glades,
Joins willing woods, and varies shades from shades,
Now breaks, or now directs, the intending lines,
Paints as you plant, and as you work, designs.

Begin with sense, of every art the soul,
Parts answering parts, shall slide into a whole,
Spontaneous beauties all around advance,
Start, even from difficulty, strike, from chance;
Nature shall join you; time shall make it grow
A work to wonder at—perhaps a Stowe.

ALEXANDER POPE, *Of Taste* (1731)

IN THE EIGHTEENTH CENTURY Stowe was the principal seat of the Grand Whiggery, the geographical and artistic centre of the cult of humane and political liberty which had its basis in the Glorious Revolution of 1688. The owners of Stowe and a network of cousins and nephews were a redoubtable force in the political life of the country for over a century. The development and aggrandisement of Stowe was intimately connected with the political fortunes and aspirations of the Temple-Grenville family and their hereditary pursuit of a ducal coronet, an ambition finally attained in the reign of George IV.

The family was among the prime supporters and beneficiaries of the political settlement which placed the Hanoverians, in the person of George I, on the throne of Great Britain and Ireland in 1714 and brought the Whigs to power for over half a century. They were the political party who sought to curtail the power of the Crown, to uphold the supremacy of Parliament and to maintain the Protestant succession. They believed that order in civil society was the result of a voluntary contract to establish representative authority. Their opponents, the Tories, still to a degree believed in the Divine Right of Kings and represented the Laudian High Church wing of Anglicanism. After the death of Queen Anne in 1714, the Tories were undermined politically by their association with the Stuarts, which tainted them with Jacobitism and kept them out of power. To quote the Oxford historian Basil Williams: 'Between 1714 and 1760 the English people, wearied with struggles and sated with glory, was content to stabilise the results of the revolution under a dynasty for which it had no love and accept an oligarchic system of government which for the time being seemed exactly suited to its needs.'

The key figure, until his fall in 1742, was Sir Robert Walpole, a shrewd Norfolk squire who became the first British Prime Minister and who communicated with George I in schoolboy Latin as the monarch could speak no English. The government's aim was to maintain unimpaired and even to enlarge the liberties secured at the Glorious Revolution and, in foreign policy, to preserve and extend the advantages of external trade and expansion won by the glorious victories of Marlborough's wars and confirmed at the Treaty of Utrecht in 1713; this had given Britain Gibraltar and a monopoly of the lucrative slave trade, and contrived a balance of power in Europe. In 1718, Britain successfully went to war with Spain to prevent her recovering the Two Sicilies (the island of Sicily and southern Italy) in contravention of the Treaty of Utrecht.

The Whigs were not a monolithic party but rather a coalition of different factions, revolving around great families like the Spencers

Begun in 1746, and possibly designed by Richard Grenville-Temple himself, the Temple of Concord and Victory was inspired by the Maison Carrée at Nimes. It was completed and re-named to mark the victorious conclusion of the Seven Years' War and the triumph of British arms in North America, India and the West Indies.

Portrait of Richard
Temple, Viscount
Cobham, the creator of
the Stowe landscape, by
Jean-Baptiste Van Loo.

or Russells. They were kept together by Thomas Pelham, Duke of
Newcastle, the Great Whig Fixer, a genius at electoral management
to successive ministries. He settled the majorities in all the elections
and kept the Whig coalition in being by means of the judicious
distribution of bribes and honours. The first half of the eighteenth
century was the golden age of Parliament. Though with a very
limited electorate, judged by modern standards, it was nevertheless
susceptible to public opinion and was representative of the true
powers in the country: landowners, lawyers and merchants. It
considered itself the equivalent of the Roman Senate and its debates
were conducted with a dignity, and rose on occasion to heights of
oratory, never seen before or since. It was in this forum that the

Temple-Grenvilles of Stowe expended much of their time and effort and where they built themselves into a formidable inner faction within the Whig party. In domestic politics they were keen defenders of liberty, as they saw it. But perhaps their most evident corporate characteristic was their strong individual outlook on foreign policy and it was over this that they diverged from Walpole.

Walpole's government, while remarkably successful in the domestic arena, reducing taxes and stimulating the economy, was less successful abroad and left England without an overseas ally; it appeared to have strengthened the Bourbon powers, especially France, England's traditional enemy. The aim of the Stowe faction was to rectify this and to extend Britain's colonial empire at the expense of her Continental rivals. The War of the Austrian Succession (1739–46) was indecisive in settling the world struggle between England and France. But the Seven Years' War (1756–63) left Britain in control of India and North America, dominant in the West Indies, and mistress of the oceans, while France was restricted more or less to a European role and Spain reduced to negligible significance. The great garden at Stowe is, to an extent, a reflection of this national achievement.

The Stowe estate had been acquired by the Temple family in the sixteenth century. As with many of the new Midlands gentry of that time – the Spencers of Althorp, for instance – their wealth was based on sheep farming. In the seventeenth century they were created baronets and produced several figures of distinction. Sir Peter Temple, squire of Stowe, supported Cromwell and served as a colonel in the parliamentary army, the first manifestation of the 'liberal' sympathies which were to develop into strong Whiggery in the following century. Sir Peter's cousin, Sir William Temple, was a diplomat, essayist and gardener. Sir Peter's son, Sir Richard Temple, 3rd Baronet, added to the family fortunes and between 1678 and 1683 built a new house in the Caroline manner at Stowe on a slightly different site from the existing building, with terraces to the south, and a wooded park to the north. This was the beginning of the great mansion and vast gardens which his descendants were to develop over the course of the next century into one of the half dozen grandest seats in all Britain.

The Temple family was raised to greatness and Stowe transformed into the most famous showplace in England by the 3rd Baronet's son, General Sir Richard Temple, one of Marlborough's officers and a prominent Whig statesman. He was the true founder of 'the dynasty and palace of Stowe'. He was at Christ's College, Cambridge, in 1694 and he may also have spent some time reading law at one of the Inns

THE TEMPLE-GRENVILLE FAMILY

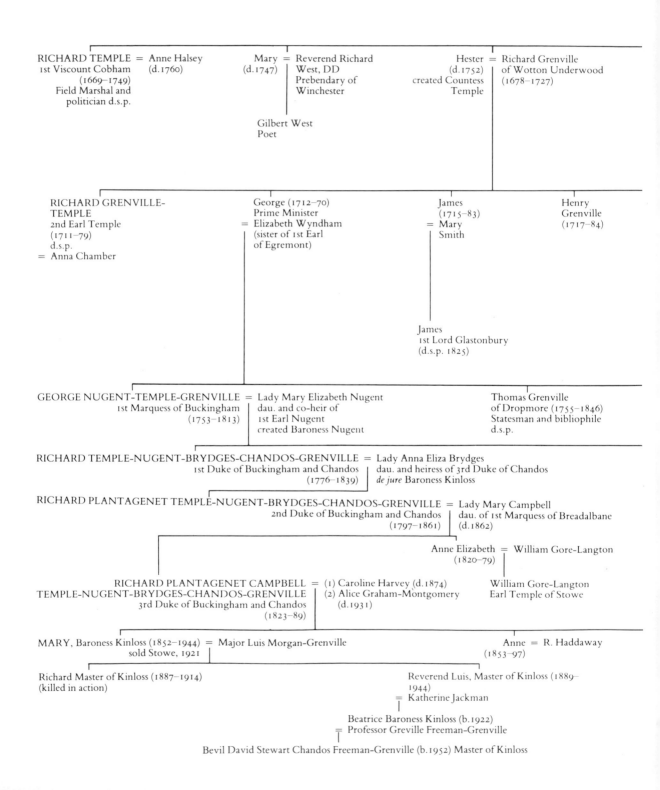

RICHARD TEMPLE = Anne Halsey
1st Viscount Cobham (d.1760)
(1669–1749)
Field Marshal and
politician d.s.p.

Mary = Reverend Richard
(d.1747) West, DD
Prebendary of
Winchester

Hester = Richard Grenville
(d.1752) of Wotton Underwood
created Countess (1678–1727)
Temple

Gilbert West
Poet

RICHARD GRENVILLE-
TEMPLE
2nd Earl Temple
(1711–79)
d.s.p.
= Anna Chamber

George (1712–70)
Prime Minister
= Elizabeth Wyndham
(sister of 1st Earl
of Egremont)

James
(1715–83)
= Mary
Smith

Henry
Grenville
(1717–84)

James
1st Lord Glastonbury
(d.s.p. 1825)

GEORGE NUGENT-TEMPLE-GRENVILLE = Lady Mary Elizabeth Nugent
1st Marquess of Buckingham | dau. and co-heir of
(1753–1813) | 1st Earl Nugent
created Baroness Nugent

Thomas Grenville
of Dropmore (1755–1846)
Statesman and bibliophile
d.s.p.

RICHARD TEMPLE-NUGENT-BRYDGES-CHANDOS-GRENVILLE = Lady Anna Eliza Brydges
1st Duke of Buckingham and Chandos | dau. and heiress of 3rd Duke of Chandos
(1776–1839) | *de jure* Baroness Kinloss

RICHARD PLANTAGENET TEMPLE-NUGENT-BRYDGES-CHANDOS-GRENVILLE = Lady Mary Campbell
2nd Duke of Buckingham and Chandos | dau. of 1st Marquess of Breadalbane
(1797–1861) | (d.1862)

Anne Elizabeth = William Gore-Langton
(1820–79)

William Gore-Langton
Earl Temple of Stowe

RICHARD PLANTAGENET CAMPBELL = (1) Caroline Harvey (d.1874)
TEMPLE-NUGENT-BRYDGES-CHANDOS-GRENVILLE | (2) Alice Graham-Montgomery
3rd Duke of Buckingham and Chandos | (d.1931)
(1823–89)

MARY, Baroness Kinloss (1852–1944) = Major Luis Morgan-Grenville
sold Stowe, 1921

Anne = R. Haddaway
(1853–97)

Richard Master of Kinloss (1887–1914)
(killed in action)

Reverend Luis, Master of Kinloss (1889–
1944)
= Katherine Jackman

Beatrice Baroness Kinloss (b.1922)
= Professor Greville Freeman-Grenville

Bevil David Stewart Chandos Freeman-Grenville (b.1952) Master of Kinloss

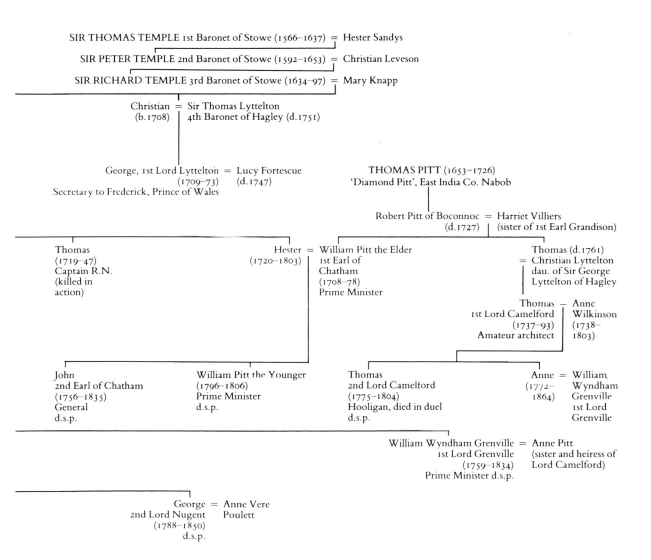

SIR THOMAS TEMPLE 1st Baronet of Stowe (1566–1637) = Hester Sandys

SIR PETER TEMPLE 2nd Baronet of Stowe (1592–1653) = Christian Leveson

SIR RICHARD TEMPLE 3rd Baronet of Stowe (1634–97) = Mary Knapp

Christian = Sir Thomas Lyttelton
(b.1708) | 4th Baronet of Hagley (d.1751)

George, 1st Lord Lyttelton = Lucy Fortescue
(1709–73) (d.1747)
Secretary to Frederick, Prince of Wales

THOMAS PITT (1653–1726)
'Diamond Pitt', East India Co. Nabob

Robert Pitt of Boconnoc = Harriet Villiers
(d.1727) | (sister of 1st Earl Grandison)

Thomas
(1719–47)
Captain R.N.
(killed in
action)

Hester = William Pitt the Elder
(1720–1803) 1st Earl of
Chatham
(1708–78)
Prime Minister

Thomas (d.1761)
= Christian Lyttelton
dau. of Sir George
Lyttelton of Hagley

Thomas — Anne
1st Lord Camelford Wilkinson
(1737–93) (1738–
Amateur architect 1803)

John
2nd Earl of Chatham
(1756–1835)
General
d.s.p.

William Pitt the Younger
(1796–1806)
Prime Minister
d.s.p.

Thomas
2nd Lord Camelford
(1775–1804)
Hooligan, died in duel
d.s.p.

Anne = William
(1772– Wyndham
1864) Grenville
1st Lord
Grenville

William Wyndham Grenville = Anne Pitt
1st Lord Grenville (sister and heiress of
(1759–1834) Lord Camelford)
Prime Minister d.s.p.

George = Anne Vere
2nd Lord Nugent Poulett
(1788–1850)
d.s.p.

Caroline Jemima Elizabeth (1858–1946)
d. unmarried

Owners of Stowe in CAPITALS

of Court. He entered the House of Commons as MP for Buckingham, a parliamentary seat which was to all intents and purposes the personal property of the family for 150 years. When the War of the Spanish Succession broke out with France in 1702, he was appointed Colonel of a Regiment of Foot by William III. He distinguished himself at the siege of Venlo, a border fortress in the Low Countries, and though not present at Blenheim, he played a notable part in several of the other major battles in Marlborough's campaign, including Lille, Malplaquet and Bouchain. He was especially prominent at the siege of Lille and was in due course promoted to Lieutenant-General.

He was an ambitious man with strong political views which he took no trouble to conceal. Swift noted that he was 'the greatest Whig in the Army'. Like Marlborough himself, he was not surprisingly dismissed by the Tories when they came to power in 1713. But the accession of George I led to a general *bouleversement* and Temple found himself once more in favour at court. He was appointed Colonel of the Royal Dragoons, created Baron Cobham and sent as Ambassador Extraordinary to the Emperor Charles VI in Vienna to announce the new king's accession. In 1715 he married Anne Halsey of Stoke Poges in Buckinghamshire, the daughter and

Jacques Rigaud's view from the north portico in 1739 shows the statue of George I beyond the pond. It was moved nearer to the house in the nineteenth century.

heiress of a rich London brewer, and it was her large fortune which enabled him to transform the family seat at Stowe. In 1718 he became Viscount Cobham, and the following year saw the high point of his military career when he was appointed commander of the highly successful punitive expedition against Vigo in Spain (after which Vigo Street in London is named). This was his last active campaign, though he continued to be granted various commissions and military appointments. In the words of Lord Rosebery, the late nineteenth-century historian and Liberal Prime Minister, he 'was not merely a soldier who had served with distinction under Marlborough, but a fortunate courtier on whom the House of Hanover had heaped constant and signal honours'. He was created Constable of Windsor Castle, Governor of Jersey, a Privy Councillor, Colonel of the First Dragoons, and was afterwards to become a Field Marshal (in 1742) and Colonel of the Horse Guards.

Though he was said to have had some of the coarse Shandyan humour of Marlborough's veterans, portraits of him show a refined countenance and he was a member of the cultivated society which revolved round the Kit-cat Club*, where he and other members

* So called after 'Kit-cats', mutton pies, eaten at the tavern that the members initially used as a meeting place.

The Kit-cat Club, painted by Gawen Hamilton Charles Bridgeman, the landscape gardener, is in the middle of the back row (sixth from the right).

The garden at Stowe is only the nucleus of a much more extensive landscape layout which covers a wide area of the surrounding country, and includes two splendid avenues: the Grand Avenue from Buckingham and the Oxford Avenue—seen here— from the Brackley road on the west.

gathered in the evening 'to discuss politics, literature or the news of the day over a bottle of wine'. He had a keen appreciation of architecture and literature as well as being a pioneer in the art of the garden. Many literary figures were intimate friends; William Congreve, the dramatist, for instance, who in his verse *Epistle to Viscount Cobham* (1729) spoke of him as the 'Sincerest Critick of my Prose and Rhime', or Alexander Pope, who stayed at Stowe for weeks on end and in his *Epistle to Lord Cobham* (1733) wrote:

> And you, brave Cobham, to the latest breath
> Shall feel your ruling passion strong in death:
> Such in those moments as in all the past
> 'Oh save my country! heav'n' shall be your last.

James Thomson, the fashionable poet who wrote the words of *Rule Britannia*, referred to Stowe directly in *The Seasons*, describing it as a 'faire majestic paradise'. Its powerful literary associations were among the outstanding attributes of Lord Cobham's garden.

Nor did he make his country seat just a retreat for men of letters. In Cobham's time it became a centre of intense political activity, a

View over Hawkwell Field to the Temple of Friendship from the Queen's Temple, one of the principal vistas in the eastern part of the gardens. The Temple of Friendship was designed by James Gibbs in 1729 for Viscount Cobham and was dedicated to his political friendship with Frederick, Prince of Wales, son of George II.

role it was to play for nearly a hundred years, so much so that by the second half of the eighteenth century it is hardly an exaggeration to say that it was the place from which England was governed. The basis of the Stowe political connection was Lord Cobham's increasing disenchantment with the Prime Minister Sir Robert Walpole. He was shocked by the latter's handling of the South Sea Company crisis, when wild speculation in the company's stock caused widespread financial ruin. He also considered that Walpole and George II's foreign policies were sacrificing the true interest of Britain to those of Hanover by not taking a strong line against France for fear of jeopardizing the King's beloved German principality. The final break came over Walpole's introduction of Excise Duty in 1733, a tax rather like VAT which it was proposed to impose on every article of consumption, giving the Customs and Excise men powers to enter every shop and home in the country to see that it was enforced. Cobham voted against the bill. The Prime Minister responded, in Rosebery's words, with 'one of those needless affronts which seem so inconsistent with the robust and genial character of Walpole, but to the infliction of which Walpole was singularly prone'; he deprived Lord Cobham (for the second time in his life) of his regiment. 'Stung to political ardour by this insult [Cobham] began to form a faction of violent opposition of which his nephews and friends were the nucleus. Thus began that formidable influence which had its home and source at Stowe for near a century afterwards.'

Cobham's family circle thereby became a secessionist party within the Whigs, and immediately rallied round Frederick, Prince of Wales in opposition to George II and the court. They were known as 'the Boy Patriots', because of their strong views on foreign policy, or more derogatorily as 'Cobham's cubs', for their nucleus was the network of his nephews, in-laws and cousins, most of them in their twenties: the Lytteltons of Hagley Hall, Worcestershire (his youngest sister Christian married Sir Thomas Lyttelton, whose son George was secretary to Frederick, Prince of Wales), the Wests (his eldest sister Mary married the Reverend Richard West), and above all the Grenvilles and Pitts. The latter family was descended from Thomas, 'Governor' Pitt, a nabob who made his fortune in India and brought home on his retirement what was then the largest known diamond in the world. He sold it to the King of France for the enormous sum of £133,000 (though he was never paid in full). It became part of the French Crown Jewels and remains in the Louvre to this day. His descendants combined genius with near-madness, but produced two of the greatest British prime ministers of the eighteenth century in William Pitt the Elder (Lord Chatham) and William Pitt the Younger.

Cobham kept open house at Stowe and bade them think of the place as their own home. He himself had no children, and in 1717 he broke the entail on his property to a distant Temple cousin and made arrangements to bequeath the Stowe estate to his beloved second sister Hester Grenville and her family. Mary, the eldest, was passed over as the result of a family compact. By a special remainder in the patent of creation of 1718 his titles, too, were to pass to Hester and then to her eldest son. Hester Temple had married Richard Grenville of Wotton in Buckinghamshire, scion of one of the few families genuinely descended from a Norman ancestor. Her husband died in 1726 leaving her with five young sons and one daughter. Lord Cobham immediately took the whole family under his wing and educated them as his own. Of the sons, all were to sit in Parliament. Richard, the eldest, was destined to inherit Stowe, Wotton and the Cobham fortune and titles; George was to be a prominent politician and prime minister; James became Deputy Paymaster and father of Lord Glastonbury; Henry was appointed Governor of Barbados and Ambassador to Constantinople; Thomas, a naval officer 'of signal promise' was killed in action in 1747; while the daughter, Hester, married the celebrated William Pitt (later Earl of Chatham), who was to become the greatest statesman of the age.

The Grenvilles were not universally popular. They were very proud, very rich and very ambitious and made no effort to conceal the fact. They used their political influence to secure further honours and emoluments. 'Never indeed was family so well provided for during an entire century as the Temple-Grenvilles.' From returns furnished to the House of Commons, the radical, William Cobbett, later reckoned that the sons of Richard's brother George Grenville had in half a century drawn £900,000 of public money from sinecure offices such as the highly lucrative Tellership of the Exchequer, or from shipping fees from lighthouses, which in the eighteenth century were let to private individuals on highly lucrative contracts. Their shameless jobbery, even in an age of jobbery, made them an easy target for the criticism of opponents, but they were not devoid of political principle. Like their uncle, Lord Cobham, they were genuine patriots, ready to defend liberty when they found it threatened, and to fight to curb French pretensions; they were inspired with a vision of national greatness which was to find triumphant expression in Lord Chatham's administration and the glorious victories of the Seven Years' War. Their love of liberty was expressed above all in the abolition of the Slave Trade in the Grenville ministry of 1806 and in their consistent support for Catholic Emancipation.

In this winter view across Hawkwell Field, the Palladian Bridge is in the foreground, and the Temple of Ancient Virtue can be seen through the leafless trees of the Elysian Fields in the background.

Richard Grenville-
Temple, Earl Temple, in
an engraving by William
Dickinson after Sir
Joshua Reynolds. The
nephew of Lord Cobham,
he devoted his life to
remodelling and
completing the garden
on a princely scale.

On the death of Lord Cobham on 13 September 1749, his sister
Hester succeeded as Viscountess Cobham in her own right. Richard,
the eldest son, who had a great sense of his own worth, immediately
started to put into effect his plans for the further exaltation of the
family. As Lord Rosebery said: 'Hardly was Cobham's body cold,
Cobham his uncle and benefactor, to whom he owed everything,
when we find Temple urging that his mother, Cobham's sister and
heiress, should be made a Countess in her own right, with descent, of
course, to himself.' He wrote to Thomas Pelham-Holles, the Duke of
Newcastle, on 28 September, applying for this title. 'Even Newcastle,
the most hardened of political jobbers, was shocked at his
precipitation, and suggested a postponement, on the ground of
common decency. Temple brushed this objection aside with
contempt. He wished the thing done at once, and done it was.' The
exchange of correspondence survives. The Duke of Newcastle to

Richard Grenville-Temple (as he had become on succeeding to the Stowe estate):

> The request you make to the King of conferring a further title upon your mother, to be limited afterwards to you and your brothers, is undoubtedly a very natural and reasonable one, and I hope and believe will meet with no difficulty. The only thing I shall submit to you, and that I shall leave entirely to your own determination, relates singly to the point of time, whether it might not be as well to defer it 'till winter or some time after the meeting of Parliament, as to propose it just now, so soon after Lord Cobham's death and before you have had an opportunity of appearing at Court.
>
> I mention this purely for your own consideration, and am ready to do it just as you wish. I am the more inclined to mention it, as the King has lately had a good deal of solicitation about Peerages, &c., which in three weeks or a month may be a little forgot. I beg you would not misunderstand me; your answer to this letter shall determine me to do my best towards obtaining what you propose, in the manner and at the time you shall desire it.

Richard Grenville-Temple to the Duke of Newcastle:

> My Lord, — Nothing can be more obliging than the kind manner in which your Grace is pleased to answer the letter I took the liberty to trouble you with, and the readiness you are so good as to express, in laying before His Majesty a request which you do me the great honour not to think unfit. As to the time, since your Grace seems to make some doubt upon that, I confess I could wish that your Grace had taken me out of the difficulty of deciding that, by determining the thing yourself, because possibly some reasons for delay may occur to your Grace of which I cannot be so proper to judge; but since you have had the extreme goodness to leave me to chuse at which time I should wish an application might be made to the King in my favour, upon a matter which I have presumed to recommend to your Grace's protection, I own every reason which I conceived in my poor judgment to be strong ones, that led me so soon to ask this favour, would determine me yet more strongly to wish to receive this great mark of His Majesty's condescension and goodness, and of your Grace's countenance and friendship, as early as may be.

Richard Grenville-Temple was born in 1711 and educated at Eton; at the age of eighteen, under the care of a private tutor, Monsieur de

Lizy, he was sent on a Grand Tour of Switzerland, Italy and France. He remained on the Continent for more than four years, developing a serious taste for art, architecture and classical antiquity, and, as was the custom, got into debt to some tune. On his return, his mother and uncle desired him to get married to settle his 'distressed affairs'. To enable him to do so 'to the highest advantage, Lord Cobham publicly declared that he would settle his whole estate upon him which he accordingly did upon his marriage with Miss Anna Chamber', so his brother George Grenville tells us. Anna Chamber was the daughter and co-heiress of Thomas Chamber of Hanworth, Middlesex, and grand-daughter of Charles, 2nd Earl of Berkeley; she brought her husband a fortune of £50,000, the equivalent of about five million pounds in today's money. She had many amiable qualities, not the least of which in her husband's opinion was the great fortune she brought him, yet she had not 'the advantage of person when young'. He always treated her opinions with 'more impatience and contempt than she deserved, and did not find the least resource in her conversation. Yet when she died he was inconsolable.' Anna always showed to him the most constant devotion. She, like many of the Stowe set, was an amateur poet and her verses were printed at the Strawberry Hill Press, the private press set up by Horace Walpole in his famous house at Twickenham.

Richard Grenville-Temple was brought into Parliament by his uncle, after his Grand Tour, as Whig MP for Buckingham, a seat he held till he succeeded his mother as Earl Temple in 1752. His brother George was brought into the Commons in 1742 as MP for Buckinghamshire and with William Pitt, who married their only sister, Hester, they formed a closely-knit brotherhood or confraternity. Temple became First Lord of the Admiralty in the Administration formed by Pitt in November 1756 and in the following June he was made Lord Privy Seal. In December 1758 he was constituted Lord-Lieutenant of Buckinghamshire. During the greater part of Pitt's administration he played an active part in the government, being trusted by Pitt to carry on with business while the latter was intermittently indisposed by long and debilitating attacks of gout. The Seven Years' War, and his management of it 'was the chief occasion of Mr Pitts' being so much distinguished, so his intimate connection with [Lord Temple] was the principal cause why this peer became so conspicuous and celebrated'.

Despite the fact that George II detested him, Lord Temple used his family's seemingly all-powerful position during Pitt's ministry to press in 1759 for the Garter, the senior order of chivalry and the honour most prized by eighteenth-century politicians who already

The Grenville Column at the top of the Elysian Fields commemorates Lord Temple's younger brother Thomas Grenville, who was killed in action fighting against the French off Cape Finisterre in 1747. On top stands a statue of Poetry pointing to a scroll inscribed in Latin: 'Of none but heroic deeds I sing'.

enjoyed the possession of a peerage. Not surprisingly the King refused. So Pitt was brought into play and wrote a 'note full of sombre menace' demanding the Garter for Temple. Still the King refused. 'Then the last reserves were brought into play. Temple resigned the Privy Seal on the ground that the Garter was denied. Pitt had at the same time a peremptory interview with Newcastle.' The King had to yield but could not disguise his anger. Newcastle, the other chief minister in the government whose assiduous lobbying and distribution of honours had held the different factions of the Whigs together since the Hanoverian succession, wrote in his emollient way to Temple on 31 January 1760 to convey the glad tidings:

> My dear Lord, — I have too much pleasure in the justice which His Majesty has this day done to himself and to your Lordship, to delay one moment expressing my sense of it. I have long most ardently wished that His Majesty would do what was so right for his own honour and interest.
>
> My wishes are now completed, and I am extremely happy. I most sincerely congratulate your Lordship upon it, and am, with the greatest truth and respect, my dear Lord, your most obedient and most affectionate humble Servant,
>
> HOLLES NEWCASTLE

When it came to the investiture, however, George II made no attempt to conceal his aversion for the new knight or his annoyance at having been compelled in consequence of political arrangements 'very repugnant to his feelings' to grant Temple the Order of the Garter. Sir Nathanial Wraxall, the writer, MP, and traveller, tells us in his *Memoirs* what happened at St James's Palace: 'The King took so little pains to conceal his aversion both to the individual and to the act, that instead of placing the ribbon decorously over the shoulder of the new Knight, His Majesty, averting his head, and muttering indistinctly some expressions of dissatisfaction, threw it across him, and turned his back at the same instant in the rudest manner . . .', as if he were tossing a bone to a dog. Lord Temple, however, was satisfied and proceeded to splash the Garter all over his architectural embellishments at Stowe, beginning with large carved panels on the gatepiers of the new Oxford Lodge and concluding with the plasterwork of the state bedroom, and he wore his Garter Star even when sitting on a bench in the garden at Stowe in the middle of the day.

At the accession of George III in 1760, Lord Temple continued to serve as Lord Privy Seal and to support his brother-in-law; they both resigned as a gesture of solidarity in October 1761 upon the question of war with Spain. This led to a temporary estrangement from his brother George Grenville, who remained in office and adhered to Lord Bute, George III's former tutor and the new Prime Minister. Lord Temple became one of the most active leaders of the opposition to Lord Bute, and openly supported and encouraged the MP John Wilkes in his fight to defend the freedom of the Press.

John Wilkes had an estate in Buckinghamshire by right of his wife and was MP for Aylesbury. He was a supporter of William Pitt and a member of the anti-Bute Stowe set, helping Lord Temple to organize the Buckinghamshire Militia in which he served as a colonel. He carried on an anonymous pamphlet campaign against the new government's foreign policy, in which he promulgated the Pitt-Grenville view. In 1762 he founded the *North Briton*, an ironical political paper, the first issue of which on 5 June included a scathing attack on Lord Bute. Subsequent issues continued to harry the government and culminated in April 1763 in an attack on the King himself. The government decided to treat this as a seditious libel, but as the publication was anonymous they could not issue a regular warrant

OVERLEAF
The Oxford Bridge in the early morning.

The Oxford Lodge. The gate piers designed by William Kent were moved to their present site in 1761 and embellished with the insignia of the Garter which Lord Temple went to such lengths to obtain.

for Wilkes's arrest. He was arrested nevertheless under the doubtful legality of a general warrant. Lord Temple applied for Habeas Corpus on Wilkes's behalf and had him released. Lord Bute responded by dismissing Lord Temple from his post as Lord-Lieutenant of Buckinghamshire and had Wilkes's house searched and his private papers taken. Such an action while the House of Commons was sitting was a serious infringement of the privileges of an MP. Wilkes sued the government and was awarded £1000 damages. He then continued his attacks in the *North Briton* till the government brought the seditious libel action to court, whereupon Wilkes travelled to the Continent while the lengthy case worked itself out; he eventually returned to take up his seat in Parliament to cries of 'Wilkes and Liberty'. Throughout this period both his legal expenses and his subsistence in France and Italy were paid by Lord Temple.

In this episode Lord Temple proved himself on the side of the angels and a sound champion of Liberty as it was upheld at Stowe. In retaliation Bute dismissed him from his post as Lord-Lieutenant of Buckinghamshire. This slight seems to have acted as a further spur to

The Buckingham Lodges flank the entrance to the Grand Avenue. Their design is attributed to Vincenzo Valdrè and they are embellished with Coade stone reliefs and fragments of ancient sarcophagi.

his ambition; he was not content with being an earl, a Knight of the Garter and, it was said by contemporaries, the richest subject in England. As well as his uncle's fortune, his wife's fortune and his father's fortune, he had also inherited that of Bubb Dodington, a much-mocked nouveau-riche and politician who had a large Dorset estate from his maternal uncle (his father having been an apothecary). The Temples were heirs to the Dodington fortune through the marriage of Hester Temple, daughter of Sir Peter, the 2nd baronet, to Bubb Dodington's maternal grandfather. Lord Temple now began to angle for a dukedom. Thus began the grand obsession of the lords of Stowe who for three generations patiently and persistently pursued a ducal coronet, an obsession described with grudging respect by Lord Rosebery in his biography of the Earl of Chatham:

> What is really admirable indeed is the pertinacity and concentration of this strange, dogged race, and their devotion, indeed subjection, to their chief; they were a political Company of Jesus. Their objects were not exalted, but from generation to generation, with a patience little less than Chinese, they pursued and ultimately attained what they desired. They were of course unpopular, because their scheme was too obvious; but they knew the value of popularity, and attempted it with pompous and crowded entertainments. They were not brilliant; but in every generation they had a man of sufficient ability, two prime ministers among them [actually four], to further their cause. They built, no doubt, on inadequate foundations, but these lasted just long enough to enable the structure to be crowned. It is a singular story; there is nothing like it in the history of England; it resembles rather the persistent annals of the hive.

In May 1765 Lord Temple was reconciled to his brother George, who by that time had succeeded Bute as prime minister, and they remained on the most friendly terms thereafter. In June 1765 George III tried to form a new ministry under Pitt, but found that an absolute condition of that ministry was that Temple should be First Lord of the Treasury. But then to everybody's astonishment, Temple refused on various flimsy grounds. When pressed what these were Temple said he had 'tender and delicate reasons', but did not explain what. There seems little doubt that he had made the ducal coronet a condition of his supporting the government. Pitt obviously thought this was going too far and formed the government on his own, which led to a quarrel between himself and Temple, healed only shortly before Pitt's death. Temple himself withdrew from public life and devoted his last years to the improvement of Stowe, where the cantankerous pride which his contemporaries found so insufferable in political life was transmuted into architectural embellishment on a princely scale.

Sir Nathanial Wraxall, who visited Stowe in 1776 towards the end of Lord Temple's life, has left a vivid description of his host

> the late Lord Temple, then far advanced in life, and very infirm. In his person he was tall and large, though not inclined to corpulency. A disorder, the seat of which lay in his ribs, bending him almost double, compelled him in walking to make use of a sort of crutch, but his mind seemed exempt from any decay. His conversation was animated, brilliant, and full of entertainment. Notwithstanding the nickname of 'Lord Gawky', which he had obtained in the satirical or party productions of those times and which we may presume was not given him without good reason, he had nevertheless the air and appearance of a man of high condition, when he appeared with the insignia and decoration of the Garter, seated at table.

Another contemporary critic called him one of the 'most straightforward, honest, and honourable men of his age'. These more charitable views should be set against the, admittedly biased, strictures of Horace Walpole, who wrote: 'This malignant man worked in the mines of successive factions for over thirty years together.'

Lord Temple, like his uncle Cobham, had no children of his own and on his death, caused by a carriage accident in the park at Stowe, bequeathed the estate to a Grenville nephew, George, the eldest son of his brother, also George, who had been born in 1712. George Grenville, Senior, had been educated at Eton and Christ Church, Oxford, and entered upon the study of the Law till summoned by his uncle Cobham to support the family interest in the House of Commons, where he embarked on a distinguished political career. He was made First Lord of the Admiralty and of the Treasury in June 1747. He was Treasurer of the Navy, with some interruptions, from 1754 till May 1762 when, having attached himself to Lord Bute, he was made Secretary of State. On the resignation of Lord Bute in April 1763 he was appointed First Lord of the Treasury and Chancellor of the Exchequer. As prime minister, the principal measure with which his name is associated is the American Stamp Act which played an important part in provoking the thirteen States to rebellion in 1776. The measure was patriotic and well-intentioned on the part of Grenville, and was supported by both Houses of Parliament, but the effect was disastrous. He had the reputation of being 'universally able

George Nugent-
Temple-Grenville,
Marquess of
Buckingham, in an
engraving after a portrait
by Thomas
Gainsborough. He
succeeded his uncle, Lord
Temple, in 1779 and
added the finishing
touches to the Stowe
landscape.

in the whole business of the House', but George III was not alone in
finding his grinding attention to minutiae insufferable. Edmund
Burke, on the other hand, paid generous tribute to his integrity and
powers of application in his famous speech on American Taxation in
April 1774:

> Undoubtedly Mr Grenville was a first-rate figure in this country.
> With a masculine understanding, and a stout and resolute heart,
> he had an application undissipated and unwearied. He took public
> business not as a duty he was to fulfil, but as a pleasure he was to
> enjoy, and he seemed to have no delight out of this House, except
> in such things as some way related to the business that was to be
> done within it. If he was ambitious, I will say this for him, his
> ambition was of a noble and generous strain. If it was to raise

himself, not by the low pimping politics of a court, but to win his way to power through the laborious gradations of public service, and to secure himself a well-earned rank in Parliament, by a thorough knowledge of its constitution, and a perfect practice in all its business . . . .

No minister was ever more easy of access, or gave a more patient or attentive hearing to such as applied to him; and though he entered upon the management of affairs at the most critical conjuncture, with many and great prejudices on certain accounts against him, yet his steady, upright, and able conduct had conciliated the minds of men to him; and nothing, perhaps, could give the wiser and more rational part of mankind better hopes, and better expectations, than to see a man of these distinguished abilities, of this unwearied attention, and of this unblemished integrity, again serving his country, in one of the highest and most important offices of State.

Engraving of the Oxford Lodge by T. Medland. The flanking pavilions are attributed to Valdrè.

When speaking in the House George Grenville adopted a 'querulous, languid, fatiguing tone' which was the origin of his nickname of 'Gentle Shepherd'. It seems that he had a generally tedious manner. George III complained: 'When he has wearied me for two hours, he looks at his watch to see if he may not tire me for an hour more.'

George Grenville married Elizabeth Wyndham, sister of the Earl of Egremont, in 1749. They were devoted to each other and had a large family of three sons and four daughters. The latter made marriages into some of the 'most distinguished families of rank in the country', while all three sons continued family tradition and filled high political office. The second son, Thomas, was a statesman who negotiated the peace treaty with the United States in 1782. He also formed one of the most splendid of all private libraries, consisting of 20,000 rare books, which he bequeathed to the British Museum on his death. William, the youngest, afterwards Lord Grenville, was one of the most eminent statesmen in the latter years of the reign of George III. He was Foreign Secretary for a long period and like his father before him served briefly as prime minister (in the Ministry of All the Talents, 1806). The eldest son, George Grenville, succeeded as Earl Temple, Viscount Cobham and Baron Cobham in 1779. He was MP for Buckinghamshire from 1774 till his translation to the Lords, and was the natural leader of the Grenville faction of the Whig party. He strongly opposed Charles James Fox's India Bill, and at first supported his cousin William Pitt the Younger, playing a large part in the intrigues that brought Pitt to power. It was he, for instance, who got written authority from George III to state that the King regarded the supporters of the India Bill as his enemies, which dished the chances of Charles James Fox becoming prime minister and cleared the way for Pitt. His major political appointment was a double stint as Lord-Lieutenant of Ireland from 1782 to 1783 and again from 1787 to 1789. While at Dublin Castle in 1783 he instituted and was the first Grand Master of the Order of St Patrick, a new order of chivalry intended to be the Irish equivalent of the Garter in England and the Thistle in Scotland. Again following family tradition, he married an heiress, a charming Irish girl and a Roman Catholic, Mary Elizabeth, daughter of Robert, Earl Nugent, and he added her surname to his own by Royal Licence to become Nugent-Temple-Grenville; in 1788 he succeeded his wife's father as Earl Nugent by special remainder, in addition to his own titles.

The Grenville family pride showed no signs of abating in his person, rather the reverse. He was advanced a further notch in the peerage, being created Marquess of Buckingham in 1784, as a reward for his service in Ireland. Horace Walpole wrote of him: 'He was weak, proud, avaricious, peevish, fretful, and femininely observant of the punctilio of visits, and he had every one of these defects in the extreme with their natural concomitant, obstinacy. His wife had more sense with as much pride.' The Lord-Lieutenant's ADC in Ireland, Robert Hobart (later Earl of Buckinghamshire), wrote of him to the Duke of Rutland in December 1785: 'If pride, arrogance and self-sufficiency be qualities for a Popish minister, the noble Marquis himself, by embracing that religion which he appeared to encourage in his wife, may be at the head of the Papistical Court.' Lord Charlemont in his *Memoirs* was more generous: 'Endowed by nature with excellent abilities he rendered their effect tenfold by diligence . . . His love of business was such that he seemed to have no other passion. He did everything himself and consequently it was well done.' But even Charlemont noted that his manner was 'by no means formed to please' and that he was 'proud and too apt to undervalue his equals'.

There is no doubt that he was a man of considerable industry and some ability, especially in financial matters. But he was pompous, formal and self-sufficient and lacked generous sympathies. It is possible that the aspects of his character which contemporaries found so rebarbative were exacerbated by shyness, for he stuttered, and did not enjoy good health. Disappointed in his hopes for a dukedom and having to make do with a mere marquessate, he retired from public life on his return from Ireland for the second time in 1787 and spent his later years in isolated splendour at Stowe. George III remarked of him: 'I hate nobody, why should anybody hate me? I beg pardon, I do hate the Marquess of Buckingham.'

Like his uncle Temple and great-uncle Cobham before him, the Marquess of Buckingham was a man of taste and a patron of the arts. On his Grand Tour in 1774 he had visited Pompeii and been fired by enthusiasm for antiquity. While in Rome he had assembled a collection of classical sculpture, and on his return home he added substantially to the holding of Old Master paintings, rare books and manuscripts at Stowe. In this he was aided by his wife, who was herself interested in art and was an amateur painter. He also continued to increase the size of the property. 'Acre was added to acre and estate to estate, often by the dangerous expedient of borrowed money, until Buckinghamshire seemed likely to become the appanage of the family. Borough influence was laboriously accumulated and maintained. Nor were nobler possessions disdained. Rare books and manuscripts, choice pictures and sumptuous furniture were added.'

On his death in 1813, the ownership of Stowe for the first time for

over a century passed from father to son. His eldest son, Richard, was born in 1776 and matriculated at both Brasenose College, Oxford, and Magdalene College, Cambridge, and following family tradition was MP for Buckingham from 1797 till raised to the Lords on his father's death in 1813. Naturally, he at first supported the government of his cousin William Pitt the Younger, but in 1802 changed sides and went into opposition, becoming one of the twenty-four managers of the impeachment of Lord Melville, Pitt's friend and close colleague, in 1805. Inevitably, he married an heiress, and the greatest heiress of them all, Anna Eliza, Baroness Kinloss (in her own right), only daughter of James Brydges, 3rd Duke of Chandos. They were engaged when he was ten and she was six. By royal licence he added her name to his own to become Temple-Nugent-Brydges-Chandos-Grenville. He also added to the beauties of Stowe, collecting natural curiosities, sculpture, paintings and prints. He was among the fattest men of his generation, and reputedly the heaviest man that the Neapolitan porters had ever had to carry up Vesuvius.

It was in his time that the family ambition was finally achieved when he was created a duke by King George IV in 1824, the only dukedom to be bestowed by that monarch and ostensibly a mark of the King's special favour and friendship. But like all the previous advances of the Grenvilles, it was the result of the well-judged use of irresistible political influence. In Lord Rosebery's view it was almost a commercial compact. The Tory prime minister, Lord Liverpool, needed the support of the Grenville faction in the House of Commons if he were to remain in power. The bargain was proposed. Louis XVIII, a family friend from the days of the French royal family's exile in Buckinghamshire during the Revolution and Napoleonic period (Hartwell House had been found for him at that time by Lord Buckingham, a kindness which the Bourbons remembered), added his support, and Buckingham became a duke. Lord Holland remarked 'all articles are now to be had at low prices except Grenvilles'. Charles Bagot wrote 'I am glad the Grenvilles are taken into the Government; and (for Grenvilles) they come tolerably cheap. I see no objection to a Dukedom [going] to the head of the Grenville family, but I see many giving it to the actual blubberhead who now reigns over them.' And from that moment the star of the family visibly waned. Two more Dukes of Buckingham and Chandos were to reign at Stowe, but the foundations were insufficient, the estates, collections, and treasures were dispersed, and the male line died out. In Lord Rosebery's arresting phrase: 'The glories of the House built up with so much care and persistence, vanished like a snow-wreath.' But that story is for a later chapter.

II

CREATION OF A SEAT

Of Improving the Present Time
(1728)

Sincerest critic of my prose or rhyme,
Tell how thy pleasing Stowe employs thy time.
Say, Cobham, what amuses thy retreat,
Or schemes of war, or stratagems of state?
Dost thou recall to mind with joy or grief
Great Marlborough's actions, that immortal chief,
Whose slightest trophy raised in each campaign
More than sufficed to signalise a reign?
Does the remembrance, rising, warm thy heart
With glory past, where thou thyself hadst part,
Or dost thou grieve indignant, now, to see
The fruitless end of all that victory?
. . . Or dost thou give the winds afar to blow
Each vexing thought and heart-devouring woe,
And fix thy mind alone on rural scenes,
To turn the levelled lawns to liquid plains,
To raise the creeping rills from humble beds,
And force the latent springs to lift their heads,
On watery columns capitals to rear
That mix their flowing curls with upper air?

WILLIAM CONGREVE

MANY IN THE EIGHTEENTH CENTURY claimed that the landscape garden was an English invention — like liberty, with which it was often compared. Perhaps surprisingly, the English school of landscape design was conceived by philosophers, writers and virtuosi, not by architects or gardeners, and it owed much to the influence of poetry, classical landscape painting and the impact of foreign travel — the Grand Tour — especially in Italy with its beautiful vistas dotted with Roman ruins and overgrown Renaissance gardens. English landowners attempted to remodel their properties to form similar landscape pictures. In the words of Joseph Addison, one of the literary originators of the English garden: 'a man might make a pretty landscape [painting] of his own possessions.'

Landowners were encouraged by the writings of various moral philosophers, who stressed the superiority of Nature over the artificiality of formal geometrical garden design. Particularly influential was the Earl of Shaftesbury, who wrote: 'I shall no longer resist the passion in me for things of a natural kind; where neither Art, nor the Conceit or Caprice of Man has spoil'd their genuine order.' He claimed that 'an estate modelled to represent NATURE would be more engaging and appear with the Magnificence beyond the formal Mockery of princely gardens'. This theme was taken up by poets, notably Alexander Pope with his famous dictum 'all gardening is landscape painting', and James Thomson, author of *The Seasons*.

The idea of planting a whole estate to look like a natural landscape painting, and the laying out of beautiful contrived prospects, was made technically possible by the invention of the sunk fence or 'ha-ha', a French idea which was first used on a large scale in England by Charles Bridgeman, the royal gardener, in his great layouts at Blenheim, Kensington Palace Gardens and at Stowe itself. The ha-ha enabled the exact bounds of the garden to be concealed and thus the walks, avenues and vistas seemed to pass imperceptibly into the countryside beyond, with no sharply defined break between the two. The Stowe landscape was the earliest large-scale example of this new approach to gardening in England. In its first phase it was still artificial, and a balance was still struck between formal features like straight paths or hedges and geometrically shaped ponds and lawns; but the planting was increasingly naturalistic, with untrimmed trees and shrubs rather than neatly clipped topiary, a general loosening of the confines and an overall lack of balanced symmetry.

This new style of gardening was consonant with new habits of thought, especially the increasing emphasis on private meditation. Whereas geometrically ordered, French-style gardens in the manner of Versailles, which were previously the vogue, were intended as backdrops for large social gatherings and ceremonial occasions, the English landscape garden was for walking in. It was designed to be seen, not in one impressive gulp, but as a result of exploration, with a succession of surprises and unsuspected beauties revealed to the spectator. In an Augustan landscape garden, like Stowe, temples, statues and inscriptions were incorporated as part of the overall design and were intended to evoke the received understanding of history, mythology and literature. These associational poetic qualities were as important as the visual effects in the overall impact of the garden.

The layout at Stowe went through three successive stages. It started as a small conventional, geometrically ordered Caroline garden. It was then enormously enlarged and remodelled and transformed into the prime example of the Augustan or heroic formal landscape garden. Finally, it was softened and naturalized to create a private elysium, a totally informal version of nature improved.

The nucleus of the vast mansion and princely gardens developed by three generations of successive owners of the estate was the red-brick Caroline house with a hipped roof, pediment and cross-mullioned windows which had been erected by Sir Richard Temple,

Jacques Rigaud's view from the south parterre in 1737 shows the late seventeenth-century house as extended by Viscount Cobham, and the clipped hedges, moulded earthworks and geometrical ponds which characterized the first phase of Cobham's and Bridgeman's work on the garden.

3rd Baronet, after his marriage in 1675; the contract shows the house was built between 1678 and 1683. The architect was William Cleare, Wren's joiner, who had made the great model for St Paul's Cathedral, and the design of the house was based on that of Coleshill, Sir Roger Pratt's influential double-pile country house in Berkshire. Sir Richard demolished the old Tudor manor house next to Stowe church and chose a new site at the top of a nearby ridge from where there was a good view over the surrounding country. He also re-aligned the house several degrees so that the central axis focused on the medieval steeple of Buckingham church three miles away to the south. In front of the house he laid out a conventional formal garden with three terraces, one below the other, stepping down the slope towards the site of the Tudor house; but he left the existing walled gardens on the west side, which must have created an odd effect in such a symmetrical layout because they were set at a radically different angle from the new house and terraces. It is appropriate that the first in the galaxy of great designers to advise on garden layout was none other than Sir Christopher Wren, who wrote to the first Sir Richard in 1683 about the levels of terraces.

Celia Fiennes, who visited Stowe in the 1690s, described the gardens then as being 'one below another with low breast walls and taress walks ... beyond it are orchards and woods; on the other [north] side the park [with] rows of trees'. Among the Stowe papers, which are now at the Huntington Library, San Marino, in California, there is a set of sixteen estate and garden plans which are probably the working designs prepared for Sir Richard Temple, c.1680, and these show the layout in more detail. They give a clear impression of the circumscribed nature of the site with a public road, the 'Hey Wey', and the medieval church hemming in the eastern boundary; another road or bridle path running at an angle across the central vista about half-way down the slope below the house, which ended in a marshy stream; and the existing walled gardens and home park to the west. This was the house and garden which Sir Richard Temple, later Viscount Cobham*, inherited in 1697, and which he was to transform into the most admired seat in England, triumph-antly turning the defects into advantages. The highly original solutions which he and his designers evolved gave an element of variety and unexpectedness to the garden layout and led step by step to the first exercise in naturalistic landscape gardening.

During his early years as owner of the estate Cobham was away serving with Marlborough in Flanders and so did not have any time

---

* For convenience he will be referred to here as Lord Cobham.

Portrait of Sir John Vanbrugh by Sir Godfrey Kneller. Vanbrugh was jointly responsible with Charles Bridgeman for the first phase of Lord Cobham's garden, and designed the first of the ornamental structures.

to devote to Stowe. But when the campaigning ended, and especially after he had been dismissed from his appointments by the Tories, he found himself with the leisure to spend at his country house, and took to gardening in earnest. During the years 1711–14 the estate accounts indicate that he was busy in the garden. At this stage he made no significant alterations to the Caroline layout but added various embellishments such as new ponds and fountains. His restoration to favour on the accession of George I in 1714, his peerage, and his marriage to Anne Halsey the following year altered the scale of his thinking and provided him with extensive financial resources.

It seems likely that he called in Charles Bridgeman, as a consultant, at this stage. The accounts include a payment to 'Mr. Bridgeman's man' in 1714, which suggests that Bridgeman was already busy on the scene then. Shortly afterwards Sir John Vanbrugh, an old friend,* was asked by Lord Cobham to supervise the buildings; he was the first of a series of top-rank architects to be employed at Stowe (or the second, if Wren is included). Vanbrugh's earliest recorded visit was in 1719, but he may already have been consulted by Cobham before then. Vanbrugh had been dismissed from Blenheim in 1716 by Sarah, Duchess of Marlborough, so he would have had the time to take on other commissions. And he knew Cobham from the Kit-cat club, where they were both members. Bridgeman and Vanbrugh were also working in tandem at this time at Eastbury in Dorset for Bubb Dodington, a second cousin of Lord Cobham's.

It is plain from contemporary references that there was a clear division of functions at Stowe: Bridgeman was employed for the practical design and layout of the garden, Vanbrugh supplied some of the inspiration and designs for the architectural features and for

The view from Nelson's Seat by Jacques Rigaud, 1739. One of the Boycott Pavilions can be seen in the centre of Nelson's Walk, which runs straight ahead. Lord Cobham's new western avenue of approach is on the right, and the Rotunda at the end of the walk on the left.

---

* Lord Cobham, like the Earl of Carlisle of Castle Howard, was godfather to one of Vanbrugh's sons.

alterations to the house. Lord Perceval (later Earl of Egmont, a politician, writer and Lord of the Bedchamber to Frederick, Prince of Wales) in a letter of 4 August 1724 stated: 'Bridgeman laid out the ground and plann'd the whole.' And George Vertue, the antiquary, confirmed this in a reference to Vanbrugh 'who was most concerned with the direction of Lord Cobham's [gardens] or rather buildings because Mr. Bridgeman Gardener to the King had the direction and disposition of the Gardens'.

The first phase of work ran from c.1714 to 1720. Much was achieved in these years, but still strictly on formal lines. An axial canal was dug to the north of the house. The soil excavated was used to build mounts to terminate both the north and south vistas. Trees were planted along the eastern boundary to screen the 'Hey Wey'. The 'Abele Walk', a formal avenue of poplars, whose silvery foliage became a much admired feature, was planted along the south axis below the terrace gardens in front of the house. To the west a long straight walk was laid out along the north-western edge of the garden and named 'Nelson's Walk' after the head gardener. In 1719 two structures by Vanbrugh – neither of which survive – were under way, Nelson's Seat and the Brick Temple (later stuccoed and re-named the Temple of Bacchus); they were the first of many. 'Ye first

OVERLEAF
Like the Rotunda, the two Lake Pavilions were originally designed by Vanbrugh, but they were taken down and re-built further apart by Lord Temple as part of his scheme for thinning out the gardens and making them more naturalistic in the 1760s.

The view from Vanbrugh's Brick Temple by Jacques Rigaud, 1739. Later stuccoed and re-named the Temple of Bacchus, it is now the site of the school chapel. William Kent's Temple of Venus in the south-west bastion is just visible to the left of the obelisk.

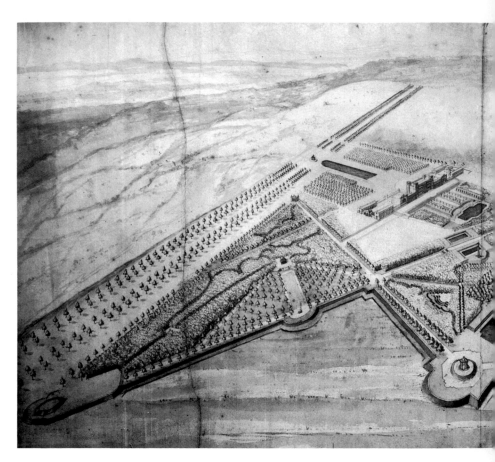

Charles Bridgeman's bird's-eye view of the Stowe layout, 1720. This shows the ingenious development to the west of the central axis, with diagonal paths radiating from the Rotunda on a sculpted mound, which overcame the then circumscribed nature of the site.

stockade ditch', the beginning of Bridgeman's great ha-ha, was dug along Nelson's Walk and the line of the Lime Walk, which branched off in a south-easterly direction, in the same year, 1719.

Vanbrugh had visited Stowe in June 1719 and reported that Cobham was 'much entertain'd with (besides his Wife) the Improvements of his House and Gardens'. Cobham's promotion to a viscounty, and his appointment as commander of the Vigo expedition encouraged him to undertake ever more spectacular projects at Stowe. It is likely that Vanbrugh's visit was to discuss the huge scheme Cobham now had in mind and which he began the following year, after his return from Spain. Between 1720 and 1724 Cobham transformed the gardens at Stowe on a completely new scale. Bridgeman produced a brilliant master-plan for the whole of the western area, (preserved in the form of a bird's-eye view in the Bodleian Library at Oxford). The accounts show that the huge reconstruction programme was launched in the autumn of 1720, and

Lord Perceval reported in August 1724 that the gardens were 'almost finished' and that Stowe had already 'gained the reputation of being the finest seat in England'.

The problem that faced Bridgeman was how to draw the disparate parts of the garden together and to create a coherent formal layout within such an irregular and constricted frame. The central vista to the south was capable of being prolonged almost indefinitely, but could not be developed with any complexity because of the public road along its eastern boundary. The new western garden along Nelson's Walk was also capable of further development, but between it and the central area lay the heavy clay pasture of the home park. Sir Richard Temple's formal garden in front of the house seemed old-fashioned and too enclosed. All these snags were overcome in the new design. The walled gardens and little terraces in front of the house were thrown together to make one large parterre. Beds of 'oderous flowers' were enclosed by hedges clipped into 'verdant arches' in which were set alternately gilded vases and statues of Apollo and the Muses. The mount at the south end of the poplar avenue was swept away and replaced by a large octagon pond containing a *guglio* or fountain, designed by Vanbrugh in the form of a steep pyramid or obelisk with water running down the sides; and beyond, a pair of Roman Doric temples, the Lake Pavilions, also designed by Vanbrugh, framed the avenue planned up the opposite slope. A similar interest was given to the focus of the north axis, by erecting an equestrian statue of George I on top of the mount at the end of the rectangular canal there. This was cast in lead by John Nost the Elder, a sculptor of Flemish origin who became famous for his lead garden statuary which adorned some of the most important layouts of the day, including Melbourne Hall (Derbyshire), Hampton Court, Castle Howard (Yorkshire) and Wrest Park (Bedfordshire). He supplied similar equestrian statues of George I for Grosvenor Square in London and the Essex Bridge in Dublin, but that at Stowe is the only survivor in situ. (The Dublin version is now at the Barber Institute in Birmingham.) It was an appropriate tribute to the king to whom Lord Cobham owed his advance in the world. The statue was later moved closer to the forecourt, but survives as the oldest of Stowe's garden ornaments.

Bridgeman's master-stroke was to tie the whole layout together by imposing a system of linked walks and vistas, meeting at a new focus to the west. By these means there emerged an unusual geometric pattern. The obstructive old garden walls on the south-west side were partly demolished. The Lime Walk was extended right across the layout from Nelson's Walk to the western boundary, parallel to the line of the diagonal bridle road across the site which had been closed. The new path was called the Great Cross Walk. Two other diagonal walks were formed: one running north-west from the Octagon Pond (Gurnet's Walk), the other, named Roger's Walk after another gardener, south-east from the north end of Nelson's Walk. (The naming of features after his gardeners was an idea Lord Cobham derived from Pliny.) Where they met near the 'Hog Pond' in the centre of the home park, a geometrical mound was thrown up and crowned with a domed Rotunda designed by Vanbrugh, which thereby became the principal focus and vantage point of the garden. The expedient of long diagonal walks overcame the constrictions of the site, and the feeling of space was enhanced by the novel use of ha-has, so that it was not clear to the viewer where the exact boundaries ran. Lord Perceval was much taken by these devices when he visited Stowe in 1724: 'What adds to the bewty of this garden is, that it is not bounded by walls but by a Ha-hah, which leaves you the sight of a

OVERLEAF
The ha-ha devised by
Charles Bridgeman is one
of the earliest and
grandest to survive. It
encloses the whole 400
acres of the garden like a
military earthwork.

The statue of George I in
the north forecourt was
cast by John Nost the
Elder and erected by
Viscount Cobham in
grateful tribute to the
king to whom he owed
his title and political and
military position.

bewtifull woody Country and makes you ignorant how far the high
planted walks extend ... The Gardens, by reason of the good
contrivance of the walks, seem to be three times as large as they are.
They contain but 28 acres, yet took us up two hours. It is entirely
new, and tho' begun eleven years ago, is now almost finished. From
the lower end you ascend a multitude of steps ... to the Parterre, and
from thence several more to the house, which standing high
comands a fine prospect. One way they can see 26 miles ... Nothing is
more irregular in the whole, nothing more regular in the parts,
which totally differ, one from the other. This shows my Lords good
tast, and his fondness to the place appears by the great expence he has
been at ... I doubt not but much of his wifes great fortune has been
sunk in it.'

Though composed of formal vistas and straight lines, the Stowe
garden had, therefore, already departed from the strict symmetry of
the baroque garden. This adaptation of the layout to suit the natural

configuration of the site, plus the use of ha-has to open up views to the 'bewtifull woody Country' show that Lord Cobham and his designers were already moving away from the conventional formal garden to something more original. The use of the line of the bridle path in the Great Cross Walk, despite the fact that it was at a markedly different angle from the rest of the layout, also shows a willingness to include an irregular feature if it made a good visual effect. This parallels the contemporary conversion by Vanbrugh and the Earl of Carlisle of the old Henderskelfe lane at Castle Howard to create the undulating grass walk to the Temple of the Four Winds at the corner of Wray Wood.

These innovations were developed further in the next stage of the western layout. The heavy clay pasture of the home park was virtually unimprovable, so it was decided to leapfrog it and to make a new boundary walk along the west side to join up with an extension of Nelson's Walk on the north side. This left the 'gadding heifers' grazing in the middle, and to prevent them from straying into the walks the existing system of ha-has was further developed. As originally conceived, the inner ha-ha was a 'stockade ditch', with sharpened stakes embedded in the turf wall according to a military principle. The new west walk was densely planted and intended to be dotted with structures which could all be seen from the Rotunda across the rustic foreground; first to be constructed was a sixty-foot high pyramid, designed by Vanbrugh. This was his last work at Stowe, for he died in March 1726. Lord Cobham turned it into his

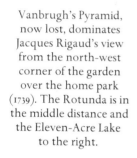

Vanbrugh's Pyramid, now lost, dominates Jacques Rigaud's view from the north-west corner of the garden over the home park (1739). The Rotunda is in the middle distance and the Eleven-Acre Lake to the right.

memorial and inscribed it in Latin: 'Among the great number of buildings designed by Sir John Vanbrugh in these gardens Cobham wished this Pyramid to be sacred to his memory.'

The progressive development of the stone-faced external ha-ha all round the boundary enclosed the garden in a pentagonal framework, with bastions at the corners like a fortification by Vauban, the military architect employed by Louis XIV. This was no doubt a deliberate allusion, for it would have reminded Lord Cobham of his Continental campaigns in the Marlborough Wars. The ha-ha at Stowe is generally considered to have been the first large-scale use of the device in an English garden. An architect with a strong interest in gardening, John James, had published his translation of the Parisian naturalist Dezallier D'Argenville's *Theory and Practice of Gardening* in 1712, and this had first given widespread currency to the idea of a sunken fence and helped to popularize the device in England. Along the marshy hollow at the bottom of the home park a new piece of water was made to the west of the Octagon and called the Eleven-Acre Lake; this was no longer a geometrical pond but a large and irregularly-shaped, almost naturalistic, stretch of water. There is a novel and transitional feeling about all this part of Bridgeman's design; the line between Art and Nature is becoming blurred. In its increasing freedom and naturalism, Bridgeman's garden at Stowe was a pioneer design which gradually broke out of the straitjacket of formality, and thereby initiated a gardening revolution which was to sweep across the whole of Britain and Europe.

Like many gardeners, Lord Cobham could not stop expanding outwards. He had already decided, having completed the west garden, to create an equivalent garden to the east, so that the central axis would be just that, and the layout would no longer be so lopsided. The ha-ha along the south boundary of the garden was extended in a straight line for 3000 feet, but in order to expand eastwards it was necessary to close the public road from Buckingham which ran up a shallow valley on this side of the garden to the church and the main entrance to Stowe House itself. If this road were to be closed, it was first necessary to make a new approach to the house from the west. Lord Cobham did so, planting a conventional formal avenue of elms (now replaced with limes) along the line of the old Roman road parallel to Nelson's Walk, but entering the north forecourt at an angle, rather than on the central axis.

This asymmetrical feature dictated by the site was developed by Lord Cobham because he liked the surprise effect. In 1724 Vanbrugh told his prime architectural patron, the Earl of Carlisle (for whom he was designing Castle Howard), that Lord Cobham favoured the expedient of an indirect approach in situations where an axial approach would have appeared 'difficult and unreasonable'. Vanbrugh reported that Cobham had told him that 'he had seen [it] done to a great Palace in Germany and [it] had, he thought, an admirable good effect'. As elsewhere in the first phase of development at Stowe, therefore, Cobham was prepared to accept a 'reasonable' expedient, rather than try to impose a strictly geometrical design on a difficult site, and thus found himself creating a novel layout. He was willing to forego an axial line of approach just as he was prepared to do without total symmetry. This was an example of the desire to 'consult the genius of the place' which Pope advocated; it shows a common-sense attitude that was beginning to modify the rule of strict formality and would soon have a dramatic impact on the further development of the garden at Stowe and lay the foundations of the English landscape movement.

The death of Vanbrugh in 1726 meant that Lord Cobham needed another architect for his buildings. On Bridgeman's recommendation, he perhaps surprisingly chose James Gibbs, a Tory, who paid his first visit in the same year. Gibbs was responsible for the pavilions, or lodges, at the new western entrance to the park, a pair of rusticated cubes with tall pedimented arches known as the Boycott

Jacques Rigaud's engraving of 1739 shows Gibbs's domed temple in its original position. It was later moved to the north-east corner of the garden and renamed the Fane of Pastoral Poetry.

ABOVE
James Gibbs's design for
the Boycott Pavilions
shows the original
pyramidal roofs, replaced
by domes to Borra's
design in the 1760s.

LEFT
James Gibbs by J. M.
William. Gibbs was
introduced to Lord
Cobham by Charles
Bridgeman following
Vanbrugh's death, and
was responsible for the
design of several of the
major buildings in the
east part of the garden,
notably the Gothic
Temple.

Pavilions*, they derive their name from a vanished hamlet nearby.
The pavilions are now domed, but originally they carried pyramidal
steeples, a much more baroque effect, and they made an appropri-
ately grand entrance to the great domain which Stowe had by then
become. Only one of them was built with accommodation, as a
house for Major Sam Speed, one of Cobham's veterans from the

* Gibbs's design is in the Ashmolean Museum at Oxford, and was also illustrated in
his *Book of Architecture* (1728).

Marlborough Wars; the other was open and entirely for effect, but it, too, has been converted into a house in recent years. Gibbs also designed a domed temple on the far side of the home park, facing the Rotunda. It was embellished with busts by the Flemish sculptor, John Michael Rysbrack, who came to England in 1720 with a recommend-ation to Gibbs. As a result, Gibbs employed him on several of his works and thus helped to establish Rysbrack as the acknowledged head of his profession in this country. George Vertue (the antiquary) wrote that Rysbrack's work was 'beautifully and masterly done, admired by all artists, and lovers of art', while Horace Walpole described him as 'the greatest master these islands have ever seen since Le Sueur'. Rysbrack continued to be employed by Lord Cobham to embellish the gardens at Stowe, but not all the statuary he provided remains there now.

> Around thy Building Gibbs, a Sacred Band
> of Princes, Patriots, Bards, and Sages Stand

wrote Gilbert West, one of Temple's nephews, in his poem on Stowe*.

Sculpture as well as architecture played an important part in Lord Cobham's garden. In addition to the statue of George I, there was also one of Queen Caroline, supported on four Ionic columns, both of which survive, but a sculpture of Prince George (later George II) on top of a column has gone. The Rotunda sheltered a gilded statue of Venus, patroness of gardens as well as goddess of love. Lord Perceval referred to 'statues cast from Anticks'. Before it was moved to the west garden, the statue of Queen Caroline crowned an amphitheatre of moulded earth ramps opposite the Rotunda, facing down a small canal made out of the old 'Hog Pond'. It was ornamented round about with statues of shepherds and nymphs. The Queen's attendants disappeared long ago, but some are shown in the illustrations of the garden made by Jacques Rigaud in 1733. These were published in 1739 by Sarah Bridgeman as a posthumous tribute to her husband, who died in 1738, though he had ceased to work at Stowe some years before. The plans are a good record of Lord Cobham's garden in its first state. Its appearance was far more architectural than the existing garden, with several geometrical reflecting-pools and fountains, and with different levels defined by sculpted earth banks and ramps, or flights of stone steps. The vistas

Lord Cobham's garden ornaments at Stowe included several grateful allusions to the Hanoverian Royal Family. This statue of Queen Caroline, consort of George I, stands on an unusual plinth of four fluted Ionic columns; it was originally placed in an amphitheatre, but now surveys the western lawns from the boundary plantation.

---

* The Gibbs temple was later moved to the north-east corner of the garden and re-erected as the Fane of Pastoral Poetry, while Rysbrack's busts were re-used in the Temple of British Worthies; the site in the west garden was taken by a monument to Queen Caroline, consort of George II.

were much narrower and neater, with gravel paths tightly enclosed in clipped hedges, backed by trees. Contemporaries referred to oaks and pines, and the light-foliaged poplar was much planted for quick effect, with underplanting of laurels. Something of the original character can be grasped by comparison with the surviving fragments of the Bridgeman layout for Bubb Dodington at Eastbury in Dorset.*

The poet Alexander Pope, who visited Stowe regularly from 1724, was delighted by what he found in 1731 when the western part of the gardens had just been completed. It was in that year that he praised Stowe as 'a Work to wonder at' and admonished other owners not to forget nature.

The most interesting aspect of the early development of the garden at Stowe was, as Christopher Hussey expressed it in *Country Life*, 'the increasing extent to which Lord Cobham and Bridgeman came to respect, and turn to visual purpose, accidents of terrain and contour, moving from geometrical grandeur to visual empiricism', an approach which was to find full expression in the eastern half of the garden as developed from the 1730s onwards.

Following the opening of the new western approach, the Hey Wey was closed, and all the area to the east of the central axis was enclosed. It seems likely that the outline of the future garden on that side was laid out in an embryonic form by the early 1730s, with the ha-ha carried round, and a bastion formed in the south-east corner to balance that on the south-west. The central portion, 'Hawkwell Field', was treated as a pendant to the home park with straight gravel walks round the boundary, and cattle grazing in the middle. The bones of this part of the garden could have been evolved by Bridgeman before he disappeared from the scene c.1733, but its detailed execution was to be very different from anything so far achieved at Stowe, with William Kent playing a prominent role.

Kent had first made his appearance at Stowe in the late 1720s, though the exact date of his initial visit is not known. He was probably first employed to advise on alterations to the house, for already the mansion itself was having to be constantly enlarged and made more impressive in order to keep up with the improvements to the grounds, an amusing situation which was to persist for most of the century. In this Stowe was the reverse of the usual circumstance where the owner built a splendid house, and then improved his grounds to match. At Stowe the garden always came first in its

The Temple of Venus across the Eleven-Acre Lake. Occupying the south-east bastion in Bridgeman's ha-ha, the Temple of Venus was designed by William Kent in 1729. The interior was originally decorated by Francesco Sleter with indelicate murals from Spenser's *Faerie Queene*, now lost.

* Vanbrugh's great house at Eastbury was demolished all but for one wing after being inherited by Lord Temple, who had no use for it, but Bridgeman's garden partly survives.

Portrait of William Kent
by B. Dandridge. Kent
played an important part
in the evolution of the
Elysian Fields and
designed the buildings
there as well as elsewhere
in the gardens.

owners' interests and set the pace almost till the end of the eighteenth century, with the house running along behind trying to keep up. Lord Cobham's enlargement of the parterre and construction of the grandiose new approach from the west, together with the embellishment of the north forecourt with a formal canal and the equestrian statue of George I and the magnification of the south vista, had left the brick Caroline house constructed by his father looking rather like an anti-climax in the middle. He therefore set about transforming it into an up-to-date Palladian mansion, adding corner towers on the model of Wilton House near Salisbury and a giant portico on the entrance front well-matched in scale to the new approach and layout. He also painted and stuccoed the brickwork to look like stone and flanked the old main block with subsidiary courtyards and ranges of outbuildings.

Inside much embellishment and decoration was carried out, including the addition of a painting to the hall ceiling showing Lord Cobham being given his first military commission in 1702 by William III. This panel was definitely designed and executed by William Kent, and it seems likely that Kent was reponsible for the other work to the house at this time. One of a pair of elegant Palladian gateways leading to the new office courts on the north front are very much in the Kent manner, though the other pair are by the Venetian architect Giacomo Leoni, who is best known for his translation of Palladio, one of the principal textbooks of the English eighteenth-century Palladian revival. Documentary evidence is lacking for the author of the north portico itself, but as well as Kent it has been attributed variously to Vanbrugh and Leoni. Kent's role was not confined to the mansion itself, and about 1730 he was also responsible for the design of the last two of the new temples in the western garden, the Hermitage at the side of the Eleven-Acre Lake and the Temple of Venus in the south-west bastion. The building's semi-circular plan is cleverly adapted to the geometrical shape of the bastion, while the design itself is a charmingly scaled-down version of a Palladian villa, with a pedimented central block connected by arcaded quadrant links to two little flanking rusticated pavilions. The central room was originally decorated with somewhat risqué murals by Francesco Sleter, a Venetian artist much patronized by Lord Cobham, though none of his work survives at Stowe. These murals were taken from scenes in Spenser's *Faerie Queene*, a sign of Lord Cobham's literary enthusiasms, but also an interest of Kent and the subject of his most attractive series of book illustrations. Kent's and Cobham's major collaboration, however, was to take place in the new eastern extension to the gardens, but that is another story.

III

LEAPING THE FENCE

Fair on the Brow, a spacious Building stands
Th'applauded Work of Kent's judicious Hands:
The spreading Wings in arched Circles bend,
And rustick Domes each arced Circle end.

GILBERT WEST, *Stowe*

Who, best of all Philosophers,
understood the powers of the human mind:
the nature, end, and bounds of civil government;
and with equal courage and sagacity, refused
the slavish systems of usurped authority
over the rights, the consciences, or the reason of mankind.

Inscription to JOHN LOCKE
on the Temple of British Worthies

WHEREAS THE NATURALISM of the western gardens was somewhat stilted and tentative, the detailed layout of the new eastern gardens gave scope to express the fully-fledged landscape manner, and it is among the earliest and most influential example of the genre. Each of its three main sections illustrates further developments of the new mode. It is this, as much as the huge scale and plethora of architectural ornaments, which makes Stowe a supremely important garden, the *locus classicus* of English landscape design. For within its 400 acres can be studied the whole history of the development of the Georgian landscape garden in Britain, with examples from each phase side by side; these in turn illustrate the advancing ideas of its owners, who remained at the very forefront of gardening taste and innovation throughout the eighteenth century. Lord Cobham, in particular, displayed a desire, regardless of cost, to keep abreast of fashion, and indeed to create fashion. In retrospect the progressive development of the Stowe landscape from a formal design to fully-fledged naturalism seems inevitable, but that is often the case with great works of art which were strikingly original at the time of their conception.

The date for the beginning of this new phase in Lord Cobham's garden coincides with his final break with Walpole in 1733 when Cobham withdrew to Stowe in 'opposition to the Court', and immersed himself in gardening, assisted by William Kent. This is confirmed in a letter from the gentleman architect Sir Thomas Robinson to his father-in-law Lord Carlisle in 1734, when Robinson referred to Claremont in Surrey for the Duke of Newcastle, Chiswick in Middlesex for Lord Burlington and Stowe, all 'now full of labourers to lay them out without level or line after Mr. Kent's notion'. Kent had just finished landscaping the garden of Carlton House in London for Frederick, Prince of Wales, whose keen supporter Lord Cobham had now become. The Carlton House garden created a sensation because it had 'the appearance of beautiful nature'. And this was now to be the intention at Stowe too. In addition to the aim of creating a scenic landscape, there was also a political dimension to the new work. Lord Cobham intended it as a demonstration of his liberal and patriotic principles and as a comment on the degenerate corruption of Walpole's government. The design of the eastern garden was inspired by a carefully conceived iconographical programme that incorporated political allusions as well as the more usual classical and literary references.

The first area to be tackled was the site of the old road, a narrow valley on the east side of the garden parallel to the principal vista. William Kent (who, as we have seen, had already been working at

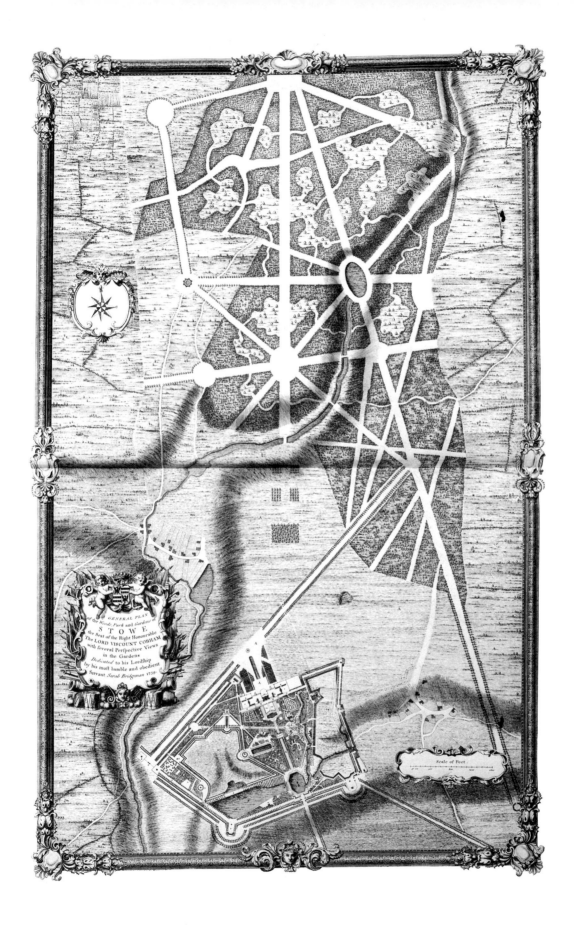

GENERAL PLAN
of the Woods Park and Gardens of
STOWE
the Seat of the Right Honourable
The LORD VISCOUNT COBHAM
with several Perspective Views
in the Gardens
Dedicated to his Lordship
by his most humble and obedient
Servant Sarah Bridgeman 1739.

Scale of Feet.

Stowe) was the governing influence here. The result, known as the Elysian Fields, is one of his finest achievements, a perfect little work of art within a work of art, comparable to Kent's contemporary garden layout at Rousham in Oxfordshire, where he created a similar arcadia for General Dormer, with a serpentine stream, temples and statues. Like the latter, the Elysian Fields at Stowe have survived with remarkably little alteration, and for two and a half centuries have been admired by visitors as one of the most attractive features of the whole Stowe complex. Though Kent was responsible for the detailed design, the programme of ideas expressed was devised by Lord Cobham and his circle, and it reflects their literary and political pre-occupations. The basis of the new garden was almost certainly an essay by Joseph Addison in *The Tatler*. Addison describes an allegorical dream where he found himself in a wood with paths running through it, full of people. He joined:

This detail from Charles Bridgeman's plan of 1739 shows the original layout of Lord Cobham's garden with the Elysian Fields and Hawkwell Field to the east of the central vista, but with the Grecian Valley still to be developed in the north-east corner (top right).

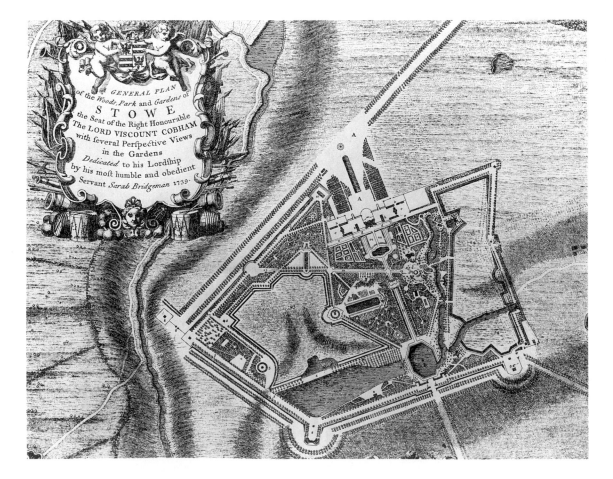

the middle-aged party of mankind [who] marched behind the standard of ambition. The great road lay in a direct line, and was terminated by the temple of Virtue. It was planted on each side with laurels, which were intermixed with marble trophies, carved pillars, and statues of lawgivers, heroes, statesmen, philosophers and poets. The persons who travelled up this great path were such whose thoughts were bent upon doing eminent services to mankind, or promoting the good of their country ... The edifices at the extremity of the walk were so contrived, that we could not see the temple of Honour, by reason of the temple of Virtue, which stood before it ....

Having seen all that happened to this band of adventurers, I repaired to another pile of building, that stood within view of the temple of Honour .... I found that the stones were laid together without mortar, and that the whole fabric stood upon so weak a foundation, that it shook with every wind that blew. This was called the temple of Vanity ... [and] was filled with hypocrites, pedants, free-thinkers, and prating politicians.

OVERLEAF
The Temple of Ancient Virtue designed by William Kent is the dominant structure in the Elysian Fields and is an Ionic version of the Temple of Vesta at Tivoli. When first erected, it was partnered by a Temple of Modern Virtue, devised as a ruin.

Here are all the features of Kent's Elysian Fields. The straight long path is the Great Cross Walk which gave entry to the new part of the gardens and was terminated by a Temple of Virtue (Ancient Virtue), beyond which was a Temple of Honour (British Worthies). Nearby was a Temple of Vanity (Modern Virtue, designed as a ruin). The statues actually set up in and around these new temples at Stowe reflected the classes of people described by Addision in his essay.

The aim was to create a 'Sacred Landscape' in the Roman manner, similar to that surrounding the Temple of Vesta at Tivoli, well known to eighteenth-century Englishmen from the paintings of Gaspard Dughet, Claude Lorraine and Nicolas Poussin. It was not for nothing that Joseph Spence referred to the Elysian Fields as 'the painting part' of Lord Cobham's gardens. Kent dammed the little stream which ran down the valley to create a chain of pools with the semblance of a serpentine river and disguised the dams as bridges. The upper dam was called the shell bridge from its decoration, being very similar to the cascades in Venus's Vale at Rousham. At the top of the valley was constructed a large grotto, the seeming source of the water; originally it had an elaborate interior but this is now lost. The river's banks were planted with a mixture of deciduous and evergreen trees to form the backdrop to the architectural features.

The key building, erected in 1736, was the Temple of Ancient Virtue, a paraphrase of the Temple of Vesta at Tivoli, but using the Ionic Order rather than the Corinthian. This beautifully propor-

tioned circular structure was ideally suited to be both the eastern terminus of the Great Cross Walk and also the presiding fane of the Elysian Fields. The domed interior contained four statues in niches, carved by Peter Scheemakers, the third of the distinguished Flemish-born sculptors to be employed by Lord Cobham on the embellishments of the Stowe landscape. They represented Greek heroes: Homer, Socrates, Epaminondas, and Lycurgus, respectively the greatest poet, philosopher, general and law-giver of the Ancient World. It has been pointed out, by George Clarke, that these figures (sold in 1921) would have been well known in the Stowe circle from the *Grecian History* of Temple Stanyan, a first cousin of Lord Cobham's, who may have advised directly on the iconographic programme. Lord Cobham and Temple Stanyan saw the ancient Greeks in the light of true Whigs, like themselves, as is made clear in the dedication of the *History*: 'It was a noble vigour with which they were animated against the first disturbers of mankind: and it is that makes them naturally have recourse to those, who have so gloriously exerted themselves in securing the liberties of Europe.'

Next to the Temple of Ancient Virtue was placed the Temple of Modern Virtue, satirically designed as a ruin (only the foundations survive) and containing a headless torso, said to be a statue of Sir Robert Walpole. The latter's son, Horace, after a visit to Stowe in 1753, not surprisingly remarked that he had 'no patience at building and planting a satire'. A similar, but more positive, comment on the degeneracy of the times was made by the Temple of British Worthies on the opposite bank of the river, so sited as to cast beautiful reflections in the water. This too was the work of Kent (1735) and is among his most attractive conceits at Stowe. It was not a new design, for he had already proposed a similar construction for the garden at Chiswick. But Lord Burlington had turned it down, and Kent was never an architect to waste a good idea. The Temple of British Worthies comprises a semi-circular exedra with curving wings containing busts in niches flanking a central pyramid. Each bust is surmounted with an elegant inscription and its own individual little pediment. Kent's source for this feature, as for many of his ideas for pictorial landscape conception, was Italian Renaissance garden design, with which he had become acquainted while studying as a painter in Italy. The particular source for British Worthies was probably the 'circus' at the Villa Mattei in Rome; there is also a similar exedra with busts in niches at the Villa Brenzone at San Vigilio on Lake Garda.

In the central pyramid was a bust of Mercury, responsible for conducting the souls of the blessed across the Styx to the Elysian

Fields. And on either side were ranged busts of those 'members of the British nation thought worthy of being set in such exalted company', a veritable Whig Pantheon. They were divided into men of contemplation, on the left, and men (plus one woman) of action, on the right. Eight of them had been carved by Rysbrack for Gibbs's temple in the west garden, and were now brought here; the others were carved by Scheemakers to complete the set. King Alfred, the Black Prince, Elizabeth I, Walter Raleigh, Francis Drake, John Hampden and William III were the patriotic men (and woman) of action. The contemplatives were Inigo Jones, William Shakespeare, Francis Bacon, John Milton, John Locke, Isaac Newton and Sir Thomas Gresham (who personified 'the honourable profession of a merchant'). On the return elevations at either end were two busts of living heroes, Alexander Pope, the poet, and Sir John Barnard, a now-forgotten MP who had voted against Walpole's Excise bill, and who shared Lord Cobham's views of the government. The finely worded inscriptions on the tablets over the busts were composed, it is thought, by members of Cobham's circle, including Alexander Pope and Cobham's nephew George (later Lord) Lyttelton, secretary to the Prince of Wales and an amateur poet. In the centre was an appropriate quotation from Virgil but omitting a line referring to priests, and it is significant that no priest appears among the national heroes; the Whig version of history is Protestant history. Lord Cobham departed from the note of high seriouness which otherwise distinguishes this part of the garden by commemorating a pet dog, Fido, at the back of the Temple of British Worthies.

The other features of the Elysian Fields were more decorative than symbolic. Near the grotto, for instance, there was a Chinese temple (one of the first in England), constructed of timber and prettily painted with chinoiserie scenes by Francesco Sleter; it was set on an island in one of the pools and approached by a little bridge. But this was dismantled in 1751 and taken to Wotton, the nearby Grenville seat (and is now at Harristown, Co. Kildare, having travelled again in 1951). The pedimented marble fountain was erected in the early nineteenth century and incorporates the overmantel of a Palladian chimney-piece from the house. It was inscribed with some contemporary lines from James Thomson's *The Seasons*, referring to Stowe and in particular to the flow of 'purest water'. Thomson was another of the literary figures who hovered around Stowe. He added a paragraph to *The Seasons* in 1744 specifically in celebration of the beauties of Stowe. In this he refers to 'Ardent genius tamed by cool judicious art' and in an aside (addressed to William Pitt the Elder) stresses the essential seriousness of Cobham's activities. His garden was not just meant to

OVERLEAF
The Temple of British Worthies is a key statement in Lord Cobham's iconographical programme for the eastern part of the gardens. It is embellished with busts of Whig heroes, by Rysbrack and Scheemakers, including representations of John Locke and Sir Francis Drake. It was designed by William Kent on the model of an ancient Roman wayside shrine.

OPPOSITE PAGE
Three busts from the Temple of British Worthies: King Alfred and Milton by Rysbrack, and William III by Scheemakers.

be pretty or even the expression of sound political principles, but was undertaken with the idea of raising Nature to the human mind and revealing ideal truth in a perfected form of landscape:

> While there with thee the enchanted round I walk —
> The regulated wild-gay fancy then
> Will tread in thought the groves of Attic land,
> Will from thy standard taste refine her own,
> Correct her pencil to the purest truth
> Of nature or . . . raise it to the human mind.

At the bottom of the Elysian fields, the chain of water along the whole south end of the garden was completed by the Upper River, a naturalistic arm of the (then) still geometrical octagon just to the west. Here Cobham erected another monument related in type to the British Worthies. This was a pyramid in memory of his old friend and drinking companion, the playwright William Congreve. Designed by Kent in 1736, it is an endearing example of his sense of humour: a carved stone monkey perched on top surveys himself in a mirror — just as Congreve held up a mirror to human nature in his comedies. The allusion is made clear in the carved inscription: 'Comedy is the imitation of life and the mirror of society'.

As soon as the Elysian Fields were completed, Cobham got to work on Hawkwell Field, the large area to the east, already enclosed by Bridgeman's extension of the ha-ha. This, too, was to be an expression of his political principles, and those of the opposition group which he was fostering at Stowe. Frederick, Prince of Wales, who had now become the focus of the opposition Whigs after quarrelling with his father George II, paid a public visit to Stowe as Cobham's guest in 1737. Partly to commemorate that visit, Cobham built the Temple of Friendship in the bastion of the ha-ha at the south end of Hawkwell Field, balancing the Temple of Venus in the equivalent western bastion. Dated 1739, it was designed by Gibbs with a Tuscan portico and a tablet with the dedication 'Amicitiae S.' — Sacred to Friendship. Inside was a banqueting room, over a basement kitchen, decorated with murals by Francesco Sleter, and lined with busts of Cobham and his 'Patriot' friends, including Prince Frederick. Thus the whole building celebrated Cobham's allegiance to the Prince of Wales, as well as providing a setting for convivial meetings of 'Cobham's cubs'. One of them, Gilbert West, wrote a long poem on his uncle's gardens, dedicated to Pope:

> To thee, great Master of the vocal String,
> O Pope, of Stowe's Elyzian Scenes I sing.

The Temple of Friendship was gutted by fire in the nineteenth century and has been a romantic ruin ever since.

OVERLEAF
The Queen's Temple from the south. Originally called the Lady's Temple and intended for the use of Lady Cobham and her friends, the temple was re-named in 1790 to honour Queen Charlotte, after her devoted nursing of George III had avoided the need for a Regency. The handsome Corinthian portico was designed by G. F. Blondel.

The interior of the Gothic Temple is painted with the heraldry of the Saxon heptarchy.

Facing the Temple of Friendship at a distance of half a mile, and situated at the north end of Hawkwell Field, Cobham built the Lady's Temple for his wife's use (later remodelled and re-named the Queen's Temple). It was probably also designed by Gibbs, and built between 1744 and 1748, but has subsequently been totally refaced. It is not known now how it looked inside when first erected. The interior was painted by Sleter with murals depicting feminine pursuits: needlework, music, shellwork and painting. Here Lady Cobham and her friends spent their summer afternoons enjoying the sunny southerly aspect.

Midway between the Lady's Temple and the Temple of Friendship, on the east side of the field, was erected the Gothic Temple or Temple of Liberty, a 'trumpet-call of Liberty, Enlightenment and the Constitution'. It is the ideological climax of the garden and Gibbs's most original and spectacular building at Stowe. Triangular in plan with three corner turrets, pointed windows and battlements, it is built of rich treacle-pudding-coloured ironstone, whereas all the other stone buildings at Stowe are constructed of creamy oolite. The vaulted ceiling of the main room is painted with the (posthumous) heraldry of the Saxon heptarchy (the early kingdoms of England), and around the outside were once ranged Rysbrack's seven marble

James Gibbs's design for
the Gothic Temple, or
Temple of Liberty'.

OVERLEAF
The Gothic Temple, or
Temple of Liberty.
Designed by James Gibbs
and built between 1744
and 1748, this is the
ideological climax of
Lord Cobham's garden
and a 'trumpet-call of
Liberty, Enlightenment
and the Constitution'.

Lancelot 'Capability' Brown by Nathaniel Dance. Brown was head gardener at Stowe from 1741 to 1751 and managed the execution of many of Lord Cobham's proposals, notably the creation of the Grecian Valley.

statues of the Saxon gods who gave their names to the days of the week: Sunna, Mona, Tiw, Woden, Thuner, Friga and Seatern — brought here from the west garden in the 1740s. Englishmen of Cobham's generation did not make much chronological difference between 'Saxon' and 'Gothic'; such nicety developed only with the rise of scientific history in the late eighteenth and early nineteenth century. To the Whigs 'Saxon' and 'Gothic' were interchangeably associated with freedom and ancient English liberties: trial by jury (erroneously thought to have been founded by King Alfred at a moot on Salisbury Plain), Magna Carta, parliamentary representation, all the things which the Civil War and Glorious Revolution had protected from the wiles of Stuart would-be absolutism, and to the preservation of which Lord Cobham and his 'Patriots' were seriously devoted. The temple was dedicated 'to the Liberty of our Ancestors'.

And over the door was carved a line from Corneille's *Horace*: '*Je rends graces aux Dieux de nestre pas Romain*' ('I thank the Gods that I am not a Roman'). The implication was that the eighteenth-century Englishman, because of his ancient liberties, was even better off than the citizen of Ancient Rome.

By the time the splendid structure had been completed, Walpole had fallen from power. As is often the way, once the unifying factor of a common enemy had gone the Patriot friends began to quarrel among themselves and one or two of the busts had to be removed from the Temple of Friendship. Some thought it rather daring of Cobham to have built a temple dedicated to friendship in the first place, and that there was a certain poetic justice in the fact that the bonds forged by politics were broken by politics.

The three temples overlooking Hawkwell Field were all bigger than anything erected hitherto at Stowe; they are all the size of individual houses. In this, they were matched to the scale of the landscape, which far exceeded that of the western gardens and the Elysian Fields. Hawkwell Field marked yet another new development in the Stowe landscape in that it was laid out as a *ferme ornée*, with a hay field in the middle and a carriage drive round the perimeter from which there were ever-changing views to the different buildings and their beautifully contrived settings. The Gothic Temple was situated in a grove of cedars of Lebanon, while the Lady's Temple and Temple of Friendship were framed by flanking plantations of mixed trees.

Where the drive crossed the Upper River, a Palladian Bridge was built on the model of that evolved by the architect Earl of Pembroke at Wilton. The Stowe bridge was the second English version of this particular architectural form. The third, at Prior Park, Bath, was slightly later.* That at Stowe, like the other buildings round Hawkwell Field, was probably adapted by Gibbs from the Wilton model. It differs in several significant respects from the prototype, principally in being set lower and approached by ramps so that carriages could be driven through the colonnade. Also unlike Wilton, the ceiling was inspired by a classical model at Palmyra, but this was a later alteration, having been inserted by Borra c.1762. The external detail is richer too, with carved masks on the keystones. When first built, the bridge marked the boundary of the garden and its back wall was solid and covered with a sculpted relief by Scheemakers. Soon after, however, both sides of the bridge were opened up, and a view contrived towards Stowe Castle, a farmhouse disguised with mock battlements to serve as an eyecatcher.

* Catherine the Great built a marble copy at Tsarskoe Selo, near St Petersburg.

Inside the Palladian Bridge. Attributed to Gibbs, the bridge is one of three versions of this particular architectural form in England. It differs in a number of details from the original, erected at Wilton in 1737 and the third, which is at Prior Park, near Bath.

By the time Hawkwell Field came to be landscaped in the late 1730s and early 1740s, Kent had disappeared from the scene, and though Gibbs stayed the course he was responsible only for the architectural embellishments. It seems likely that Lord Cobham himself was responsible for the landscape design of both this and the last part of the garden to be completed − the Grecian Valley in the north-east corner. The 1740s also saw a general loosening of the formality in the older Bridgeman part of the gardens. As the trees there grew taller, making the vistas narrower and darker than intended, they were thinned out and the surplus transplanted to the new eastern section of the garden. Some of the temples were thinned out too. As has been seen, some of the worthies and the Saxon gods were moved from the west to the east. At this time, the parterre in front of the house was swept away and replaced with a more natural-looking lawn, though the Abele Walk and the Octagon Pond still kept their formal lines, for the time being.

In these last years of Lord Cobham's life, work in both halves of the garden was carried on simultaneously, making the most economical use of his garden staff and labourers. Thinning in the west balanced the planting and embellishment of the east. Though the owner himself was the driving force behind all this, a certain amount of credit must be given to the head gardener, who was also clerk of works and responsible, therefore, for supervising both the upkeep and the alteration of the garden and the buildings on a day-to-day basis. At this stage he was one of the most famous names to be associated with Stowe: Lancelot 'Capability' Brown himself. Brown arrived as head gardener in 1741 and stayed for a decade, departing to set up on his own, with Croome Court (Worcestershire) as his first commission in 1751, after Lord Cobham's death. He married at Stowe in 1744 in the little medieval church, which was planted round with trees and shrubbery to conceal it from view, rather than being treated like one of the garden pavilions. 'Capability' Brown must have been involved in the tree-planting along the sides of the Grecian Valley, even if under Lord Cobham's ultimate direction; and that portion of the garden formed the model for his own landscape designs after he had become the most sought-after 'place-maker' in England. It was not till 1768 that he was credited with any role in the creation of Stowe, in a poem by Countess Temple who couples his name with that of Kent. But by then Brown was famous, not just the obscure head gardener of Lord Cobham. Ironically, in the nineteenth century the design of the whole garden was attributed to him.

The last part of the garden to be developed, the Grecian Valley, was begun in 1746 and was conceived as an English Vale of Tempe, presided over by a large 'Grecian' Temple, hence its name, though the dedication of the temple was later changed to Concord and Victory. It was outside the confines of Bridgeman's skeleton plan, and its grand simplicity added a completely new dimension to Stowe's expanding gallery of landscape designs. It seems likely that Cobham was assisted in his final project by his nephew and heir, Richard Grenville, then returned from his Grand Tour. There are good grounds for attributing the design of the temple itself to Grenville, not least because his portrait by William Hoare of Bath shows him with his hand resting proudly on the plan for it. His Grand Tour, and his membership of the Society of Dilettanti, a body of noblemen and gentlemen founded in 1732 to encourage the study of antique art, would have given him the necessary enthusiasm for

The Grecian Valley, the last part of Lord Cobham's garden to be completed, is partly artificial, and the estate accounts for 1746 and 1747 include payments for earth-moving. 'Capability' Brown, who was head gardener at the time, supervised the work.

The Grecian Valley, in 1946, when many of the original trees were still standing.

such a project. The Grecian Temple is remarkably ambitious, even by the standards of the Stowe garden buildings, being a 'life-size' peripteral* Ionic temple. It is based on the *Maison Carrée* at Nîmes (which Grenville had seen on his Grand Tour) and which was then thought to be purely Greek, though it is in fact Roman. The roof was put on in 1749, the year Lord Cobham died, but the interior was not fitted up until a decade or so later.

The 'valley' itself is a dog-leg-shaped declivity and is partly artificial, large quantities of soil having been excavated to create an illusion of depth. (The estate accounts include payments in 1746 and 1747 for earth-moving.) The undulating belts of trees planted along the sides enhance the arcadian effect. The first proposal was to make a lake here, and also to build a triumphal arch at the far end, facing the portico of the temple, but both these ideas were abandoned; the lake because of shortage of water, and the arch because the new owner of Stowe, Richard Grenville, has his own ideas about a more prominent site for such a feature.

At the time of Lord Cobham's death in 1749 work was already completed on a column, or prospect tower, containing a spiral staircase to a viewing platform from which the whole garden could be overlooked. This was sited between Hawkwell Field and the Grecian Valley and was built by 'Capability' Brown in 1747. It is an unusual design with no strict classical precedent, comprising an

OPPOSITE PAGE
George Bickham's plan of the garden in 1753 shows the Grecian Valley completed and some thinning and loosening, including the grassing over of the parterre, already carried out; but the Abele Walk and Octagon Pond are still formal.

* Peripteral: with a colonnade running all round the outside.

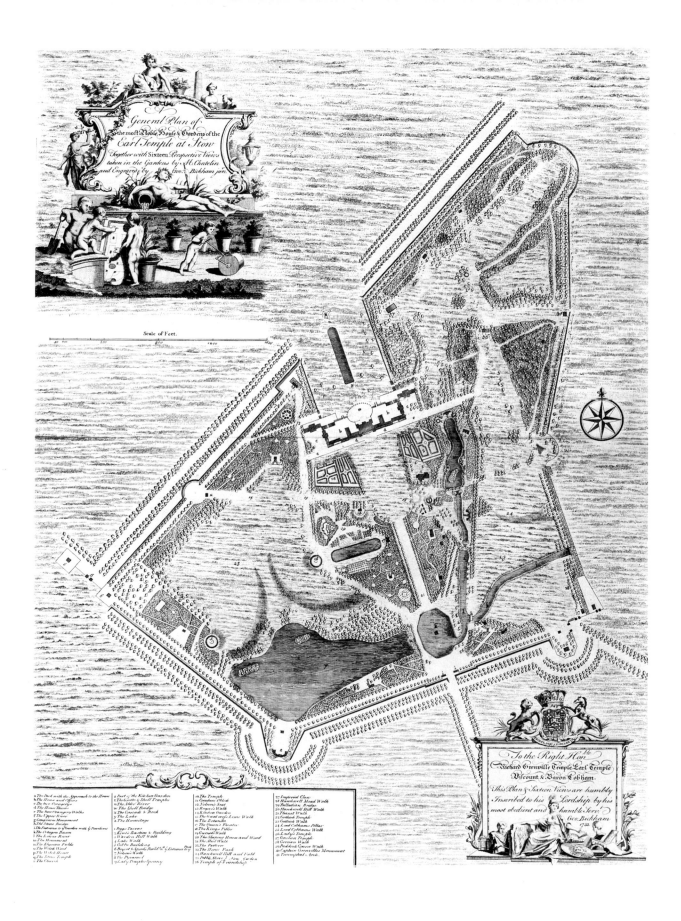

General Plan of
the most Noble House & Gardens of the
Earl Temple at Stow
Together with Sixteen Perspective Views
taken in the Gardens by Mr. Chatelain
and Engraved by Geo: Bickham jun.

Scale of Feet.

To the Right Honble.
Richard Grenville Temple Earl Temple
Viscount & Baron Cobham.
This Plan & Sixteen Views are humbly
Inscribed to his Lordship by his
most obedient and humble Servt.
Geo. Bickham
1753

BELOW
The Cobham
Monument, erected by
Lady Cobham as a
memorial to her
husband; originally it
supported his statue, but
this was destroyed by
lightning in 1957. The base
is embellished with
inscribed plaques stating
that Cobham 'saved his
country as well in the
cabinet as in the field,
and adorned it by a more
elegant system of
modern gardening first
illustrated here'.

BELOW RIGHT
This lion at the base of
the Cobham Monument
is a modern copy of the
Coade stone original
destroyed by lightning.

octagonal shaft with one large flute on each face. To modern eyes it looks more like a lighthouse than a classical column. Lady Cobham intended it as a memorial to her husband, erecting a statue on top (destroyed by lightning except for the head in 1957), and embellishing the base with plaques carrying appropriate quotations from Pope. There was also a Latin epitaph which stated Cobham's double claim to fame, in that he 'saved his country as well in the cabinet as in the field, and adorned it by a more elegant system of modern gardening first illustrated here'. The eulogy was completed with a couplet from Cicero: 'How many have imitated the magnificence of Lucullus' villas! But how few have aspired to emulate his virtues.' As George Clarke has said, in his gardening programme Cobham had displayed for fifteen years a sustained moral fervour, an insistence on scholarship, a search for 'natural' purity as exemplified in antiquity in order to evoke an imagined ideal community of patriarchal values and heroic friends. He had created an ideal landscape on a vast scale, which was also a declaration of political principles; it was intended to inspire men of action as well as men of contemplation: 'the aim of his Patriots was to go out into the corrupt world and restore its ancient quality'. This dream was to be carried into reality by the generation of Grenvilles and Pitts who succeeded.

IV

PRINCELY RECREATION

Stowe *'est un composé de lieux très beaux et très pittoresques dont les aspects ont été choisis en différens pays, et dont tout paroit naturel excepté l'assemblage, comme dans les jardins de la Chine dont je riens de vous parler. Le maître et le créateur de cette superbe solitude y a même fait construire des ruines, des temples, d'anciens édifices, et les tems ainsi que les lieux y sont rassemblé avec une magnificence plus qu'humaine.'*

Rousseau

Stowe 'is composed of very beautiful and very picturesque spots chosen to represent different kinds of scenery, all of which seem natural except when considered as a whole, as in the Chinese gardens of which I was telling you. The master and creator of this superb domain has also erected ruins, temples and ancient buildings and they, like the scenes, exhibit a magnificence which is more than human.'

B ETWEEN 1749, when he inherited Stowe from his uncle, and his death in 1779 from a fractured skull caused by a fall from his carriage while driving on the estate, Lord Temple recreated Stowe largely in the form that is seen today. It was he who gave it a magnificence which Rousseau thought more than human. In his hands the scale became immense, the architectural embellishment princely and the reputation of the garden international. He himself was in sole charge of the landscape improvements, while for the architecture he employed a succession of Continental architects – Giovanni Battista Borra, Georges-François Blondel, Vincenzo Valdrè – who served under him almost in the role of 'Court architects', as if at the *Residenz* of some European principality.

In this, Lord Temple differed significantly in his approach to the estate from his uncle Cobham, who had employed the best English architects and garden-designers at Stowe, great men in their own right like Vanbrugh or Gibbs. Under the Grenville aegis, Stowe became remarkably self-sufficient. 'Capability' Brown left in 1751 and Lord Temple brought his own head gardener, Woodward, with him from Wotton to do his bidding. He probably felt that he knew much more than his uncle about art, architecture and gardens; indeed, he had been encouraged by Cobham, who had given him the chance to design the Grecian Temple. With 'fastidious lavishness' he proceeded to embark upon the sweeping naturalization of Bridgeman's layout, and converted the whole garden into one harmonious work of art, opening vistas, smoothing contours, eradicating straight lines, softening the architectural effects, and re-asserting the predominance of the house.

By 1770 the original layout of 'straight vistas connecting nodal points and formal pools among tightly planted boskets' had been transformed and broadened till the whole resembled the character of the Grecian Valley. Great sweeps of turf were framed by clumps and belts of forest trees amidst which were dotted the many temples and pavilions as if by chance. The change in the three principal vistas is typical of what happened throughout. The lime avenue along the Great Cross Walk was 'broken' to give a more natural impression. The gravel path was turfed over. The view from the west of the Temple of Ancient Virtue, hitherto the focus of the Great Cross Walk, was planted out by a new belt of trees. Thus a formerly well-defined architectural axis disappeared, leaving behind one or two framed views in an otherwise uninterrupted sweep of lawns and trees. One of the diagonal walks meeting at the Rotunda was erased altogether, while the 'Hog Pond' canal was filled in with soil from the

Rather surprisingly, the Corinthian Arch is inhabited, and there are windows in the sides.

demolished amphitheatre, and the whole area smoothed over to give the appearance of natural contours. The Rotunda, having once been the *point de vue* of three formal vistas, was left as an isolated ornament in a now pastoral landscape.

The most spectacular transformation of all concerned the great south vista. Lord Cobham had already replaced the parterre in front of the house with lawn but left the poplar avenue – 'the Abele Walk' – and Octagon Pond. In 1762 Lord Temple felled the poplars and widened and unified the whole central vista to give the effect of a vast glade sweeping down between undulating belts of trees, and narrowing as it reached the Octagon Pond. This was naturalized, too, so as to give the impression that the Upper River, Octagon and Eleven-Acre Lake were all a continuous natural water course, interrupted only by rockwork cascades. Vanbrugh's *guglio* was demolished and its dressed stonework re-used in an obelisk to the north-east of the house over 100 feet high, built as an eye-catcher and as a memorial to General Wolfe, killed in the moment of victory on the Heights of Abraham at Quebec in 1759. The view up the opposite slope to the southern sky-line was also widened and the much broader park vista thereby obtained was defined by random clumps of trees. Vanbrugh's Lake Pavilions, which had flanked the entrance to the garden, were dismantled under Borra's direction and re-erected further apart (with some minor modifications) so as to complement the new scale. Finally, on the southern ridge a mile from the house, but on its central axis, Lord Temple erected a large

OVERLEAF
The Rotunda is the only major survivor at Stowe of a series of garden buildings designed for Lord Cobham by Sir John Vanbrugh. Originally it had a more prominent semi-spherical dome; the present gentle segmental silhouette was substituted by Borra for Lord Temple in the 1760s.

triumphal arch, the Corinthian Arch, in 1765. This was designed by his nephew by marriage Thomas Pitt, Lord Camelford, a talented amateur architect and crony of Horace Walpole's. Camelford acted as Lord Temple's architectural adviser on the projects undertaken in these years. It is symptomatic of the scale of thinking at Stowe in the 1760s that the arch is sixty feet high and sixty feet wide, yet its proportions seem perfectly matched to the setting.

Christopher Hussey described the view south from the house, the grandest at Stowe, as a coalition of the geometrical and biological conceptions of landscape; and carefully analysed the ingredients which make this vista one of the supreme masterpieces of the landscape gardeners' art. The geometrical structure, though simplified and 'over-painted', subsists in the sweeping arc (formed by turf and trees) in the foreground, and, more subtly, in the triangle in the distance composed by the Lake Pavilions and the Corinthian Arch. The biological element is provided by the way nature was summoned to clothe and soften the structure: the continuous lawn, the expanse of lake, and the park amphitheatre beyond. Each of these receding planes extends laterally, hinting at similar scenes beyond; and the framework, contracting to make the axis still relatively narrow in the

OVERLEAF
The Grand Avenue,
looking north. The
triumphal Corinthian
Arch crowning the top
of the hill frames a view
of the south portico of
the house across the
valley beyond. The
hamlet of Chackmore is
on the right.

Coade stone plaques on
the Buckingham Lodges.

middle, ensures contrasts of cross-lighting and cast shadows. 'At morning and evening the wide expanses are bright, the contracted throat dark. Chestnuts, thorns and laburnums similarly contrast in Spring with the yews and hollies, and at all seasons the noble cedars of the Kent-Brown plantings offset the rounded shapes of the hardwoods. The picture is the masterpiece in the Stowe gallery of historical landscapes, and perhaps the most beautiful, in the strict sense, of eighteenth-century English garden art.'

Nor did Lord Temple rest content with that. The enclosure of the

land between Buckingham and Stowe in the 1770s with the concomitant re-arrangement of roads and fields gave the opportunity for a master-stroke of unexampled magnificence, even though much of the land in that direction was copyhold not freehold. The old road to Stowe had wandered around by way of the village of Chackmore to the east. Lord Temple now constructed a new access road straight as a die for one and a half miles from the Corinthian Arch to the outskirts of Buckingham, and marshalled along it a great avenue a hundred feet wide planted in blocks of elm (the elms having died, the whole avenue has been replanted in recent years with alternate beeches and chestnuts). Lord Temple's Grand Avenue was as magnificent as it was singular, avenues having generally gone out of fashion by that date. It combines the impressive effect of any wide, long, axial sequence with a more subtle picturesque landscape quality, for, owing to the undulation of the ground, the approaching visitor gets an intermittent view of the distant house framed in the arch ahead of him as he proceeds along the avenue. Lord Camelford's arch thus serves a double function as the *point de vue* both of the main view from the house, and also of the avenue of approach from Buckingham. At the time it was created, the combination of a long avenue and triumphal arch at Stowe was a unique visual experience; Napoleon, for instance, did not add the Arc de Triomphe to the Champs Elysée in Paris for another thirty-odd years.

Lord Temple initiated a similar axial avenue, the Oxford Avenue, at the other main approach to Stowe, from the Brackley Road to the Boycott Pavilions. He also extended the park on that side, building a new Oxford Lodge further west at the foot of Boycott Hill, re-using Kent's gatepiers and flanking them with a pair of a little concave-roofed pavilions designed by Vincenzo Valdrè, who also designed the Buckingham Lodges at the entrance to the Grand Avenue. Valdrè (1742–1814) was the third of Lord Temple's Continental architects, an Italian decorative painter and designer introduced to Stowe by Temple's nephew and heir Richard Grenville (later Marquess of Buckingham). The new stretch of park was diversified with a naturalistic lake, the Oxford Water, crossed by a bridge built in 1761 and embellished with four grotesque urns from Vanbrugh's Temple of Sleep which was demolished at that time. The Boycott Pavilions, no longer lodges, were left as incidents on the approach. To fit them for their new role, Gibbs's pyramidal steeples were removed and replaced with shallow domes, designed by Borra, and pretty cupolas which harmonize better with the contours of the remodelled park landscape. Visitors approaching Stowe from the Grand Avenue no longer descended to Vanbrugh's temples framing the south vista –

The Oxford Bridge in winter. Constructed in 1761, the bridge's parapets are terminated with four grotesque urns, salvaged from Vanbrugh's Temple of Sleep which was demolished at that time. One of the Boycott Pavilions can be seen in the background.

the Lake Pavilions – as in Lord Cobham's time, but swept aside to the west, joining the Oxford approach just below the Boycott Pavilions, and so along the Course to the north forecourt. This too was a master-stroke of planning, for the visitor who had had his appetite whetted by the splendid Pisgah* view from the Corinthian Arch was then kept in suspense until the final denouement at the north portico. This was a perfect demonstration of the Picturesque theory that the foot should not follow what the eye had already traversed.

The part reconstruction of the Boycott Pavilions was merely one incident in Lord Temple's consistent programme to make all the architecture more suited to the mature landscape of the gardens. Sometimes this involved toning down the effects, and sometimes enhancing them. In the case of Vanbrugh's Rotunda, for instance, the prominent semi-spherical dome was taken down and replaced with one designed by Borra, with a more gentle segmental silhouette, this being considered to subsist more harmoniously with the new smooth contours of that part of the park. Later still some bands of foliate ornament were added to the tops of the columns to 'correct' their elongated appearance. In the case of the Lady's Temple, forty years' growth of the trees around Hawkwell Field had begun to dwarf Gibbs's architecture. So Lord Temple re-faced it, and added a splendid Corinthian portico approached by a wide flight of steps. As executed this bears little resemblance to the drawing prepared by G. F. Blondel which Temple had rejected.

Other buildings were simply moved around. Some smaller, frivolous objects, like the Chinese Temple, were banished altogether; others were re-sited. Lord Temple's younger brother Thomas, a naval officer, had been killed in action fighting against the French off Cape Finisterre in 1747. Lord Cobham had immediately erected a rostral column to his memory in the new Grecian Valley, near to the temple there. It is possible that it, too, was designed by Lord Temple, for its Roman archaeological overtone is just what might have been expected from a prominent member of the Society of Dilettanti. In the 1760s it was moved to the north end of the Elysian Fields, where Lord Temple must have thought that its heroic and patriotic message would be more in keeping. On top stands a statue of poetry pointing to a scroll inscribed *Non nisi grandia canto* (Of none but heroic deeds I sing), and she faces the Temple of British Worthies.

* Deuteronomy, III, 27 – an occasion that allows a glimpse of the future.

Carved ships' prows project from the Grenville Column in the manner of a Roman 'rostral' column.

The grandest of all Lord Temple's reconstructions was the house itself, which by this stage looked woefully inadequate in relation to the magnificently remodelled and broadened southern vista. The foreign architects invited to Stowe, Borra and Blondel, had been approached in the first place with this particular project in mind. Since Lord Cobham's initial remodelling, the house had continued to grow, with the addition of gallery wings and flanking pavilions to the south façade. One writer has commented that it looked 'more like a row of street fronts than a single façade'. Soon after taking over, Lord Temple had commissioned 'Signor Borra, Architect to the King of Sardinia' to remodel the house. Borra's proposed solution was to add a huge octastyle* portico in the centre, to try to pull the sprawling components together and give them a single dominant accent. This was not adopted and Borra left Stowe *c*.1762. Next the French architect Georges-François Blondel (*c*.1730–*c*.1791), son of the famous theorist Jacques-François Blondel, who was for many years professor of the Académie Royale d'Architecture in Paris, was asked to produce another scheme for a grand façade. This did not find favour either. Temple was as difficult a patron of art as he was a political figure. He treated poor Blondel with something approaching contempt and failed to pay him. In January 1774 the disgruntled architect was forced to ask the Surveyor General to the King's Works, Sir William Chambers, to intercede on his behalf. He complained of the unpleasantness of working for Lord Temple, *'qui me paye que d'ingratitude'*.

Lord Temple, too, seems to have felt frustrated by the business. In

* Octastyle: portico with eight columns on the front façade.

Robert Adam's design for the south front of the house. The several different scales of order proposed were reduced to two by Lord Camelford, who supervised the executed design.

the end he commissioned Robert Adam, *the* fashionable architect, to redesign the south front of the house. But even that great man's design did not give total satisfaction, and Temple got his relation Lord Camelford to adapt the details further before carrying it into execution, which cannot have pleased an architect as self-important as Adam. Nevertheless the result was worth all the trouble. It is a masterpiece, one of the finest classical façades in England; and Lord Temple was justified in being such a tiresome perfectionist. The new façade was completed in 1774 and perfectly complements the magnificent serenity of the great central vista. As amended by Camelford, the four Orders suggested by Adam were reduced to two – giant Corinthian for the central portico and the pilasters of the flanking pavilions, and a continuous Ionic for the linking sections and as 'mullions' for the large tripartite windows of the centre block and pavilions. The skyline was enlivened by sculpture carved by James Lovell, an artist much employed by Lord Temple at Stowe: statues of Religion and Liberty* on the west, and Peace and Plenty on the east, as well as medallions of the Seasons over the windows of the central block, and Venus and Adonis, flanked by a pair of sacrifices, on both the wings. The interior of the portico was adorned with a purely Greek Bacchic frieze copied from an engraving in Volume I of Stuart and Revett's *Antiquities of Athens* (1762) illustrating that on the Choragic Monument of Lysicrates at Athens. This book had been funded by the Society of Dilettanti, so it was well known to Lord Temple. To contemporaries it would have been an uncompromising proclamation of his refined and up-to-date architectural tastes.

* Liberty has a squint and is a portrait of John Wilkes.

OVERLEAF
The south front of Stowe from the Octagon Lake. When the development and expansion of the garden outstripped the house, Lord Temple made good the deficiency by erecting a magnificent neo-classical façade. Designed by Robert Adam, it was amended in detail by Lord Temple's relation, Thomas Pitt, Lord Camelford, a distinguished amateur.

OPPOSITE PAGE
Detail of the Bacchic frieze in the portico on the south front of the house. The frieze is copied from an engraving in Stuart and Revetts's *Antiquities of Athens* (1762), illustrating that on the Choragic Monument of Lysicrates.

Statues of Religion and Liberty from the parapet of the south front by James Lovell. Liberty has a squint and is reputed to be a portrait of John Wilkes, a political associate of Lord Temple.

The north front, too, was remodelled by Lord Temple in 1772, but in a less sublime manner. An extra attic storey was added between the towers of the main block, so as to line up with the new cornice level of the south front. To balance this increase in height and to complement the portico, Lord Cobham's curved flanking walls were replaced with taller and more graceful Ionic colonnades, and by monumental screens with niches and pilasters, to conceal the miscellaneous yards and outbuildings behind. The result is somewhat reminiscent of St Peter's in Rome. The architect is not known, but it has been suggested that the colonnades may have been the work of Lord Camelford, and that the screen walls may have been designed by Vincenzo Valdrè.

Though most of Lord Temple's architectural activity was in the nature of remodelling and thinning out, or creating new entrances at the approaches to Stowe, he added one other major structure to the garden proper. This was the Doric Arch erected in 1768, possibly to the design of Lord Camelford, between the central vista and the south end of the Elysian Fields, to which it formed a new entrance.

OPPOSITE PAGE
The Doric Arch was
erected by Lord Temple
in 1768 in anticipation of a
visit from Princess
Amelia, sister of
George III.

View through the Doric
Arch to the Palladian
Bridge. Horace Walpole
described this contrived
view as 'comprehending
more beauties of light,
shade and buildings, than
any picture of Albano I
ever saw'.

Flanking it were the re-erected statues of Apollo and the Muses moved from the old parterre in the 1740s. This arch repeated, on a reduced scale, the effect of the Corinthian Arch, for it framed delectable contrived views; in one direction across the central glade to Vanbrugh's Rotunda on the western lawn; in the other a glimpse of the Upper River and Gibbs's Palladian Bridge, with Stowe Castle in the distance. Princess Amelia, the sister of George III, for whose benefit this arch was constructed, was thrilled by it on her visit to Stowe in July 1770. And Horace Walpole swallowed his political prejudice against the Grenvilles sufficiently to praise the artful scene. He was one of the rather aged house-party assembled at Stowe for that royal occasion and left a virtuoso description of the event in a letter to George Montagu, a brilliant vignette of Stowe at the height of its glory, before Nemesis struck.

Coade stone finial based on a Roman altar on the Buckingham Lodges.

Strawberry Hill, Saturday night, July 7th, 1770.

After making an inn of your house, it is but decent to thank you for my entertainment, and to acquaint you with the result of my journey. The party passed off much better than I expected. A Princess at the head of a very small set for five days together did not promise well. However she was very good-humoured, and easy, and dispensed with a large quantity of etiquette. Lady Temple is good-nature itself, my Lord was very civil, Lord Bessborough is made to suit all sorts of people, Lady Mary Coke respects royalty too much not to be condescending, Lady Ann Howard and Mrs. Middleton filled up the drawing-room, or rather made it out, and I was determined to carry it off as well as I could, and happened to be in such good spirits, and took such care to avoid politics, that we laughed a great deal, and had not a cloud the whole time.

We breakfasted at half an hour after nine; but the Princess did not appear till it was finished; then we walked in the garden or drove about it in cabriolets, till it was time to dress: dined at three, which though properly proportioned to the smallness of the company to avoid ostentation, lasted a vast while, as the Princess eats and talks a great deal; then again into the garden till past seven, when we came in, drank tea and coffee, and played at pharaoh till ten, when the Princess retired, and we went to supper, and before twelve to bed. You see there was great sameness and little vivacity in all this. It was a little broken by fishing, and going round the park one of the mornings; but in reality the number of buildings and variety of scenes in the garden made each day

different from the rest: and my meditations on so historic a spot prevented my being tired. Every acre brings to one's mind some instance of parts of pedantry, of the taste or want of taste, of the ambition, or love of fame, or greatness, or miscarriages of those that have inhabited, decorated, planned or visited the place. Pope, Congreve, Vanbrugh, Kent, Gibbs, Lord Cobham, Lord Chesterfield, the mob of nephews, the Lytteltons, Grenvilles, Wests, Leonidas Glover and Wilkes, the late Prince of Wales, the King of Denmark, Princess Amelia, and the proud monuments of Lord Chatham's services, now enshrined there, then anathematized there, and now again commanding there, with the Temple of Friendship like the temple of Janus, sometimes open to war, and sometimes shut up in factious cabals, all these images crowd upon one's memory and add visionary personages to the charming scenes, that are so enriched with fanes and temples, that the real prospects are little less than visions themselves.

On Wednesday night a small Vauxhall was acted for us at the

Engraving of the Rotunda by T. Medland, with the Temple of Venus in the background. The newly mown grass is being raked in the foreground. The activities of gardening and farming were among the visual attractions of the Stowe landscape which were commented upon by contemporaries.

grotto in the Elysian fields, which was illuminated with lamps, as were the thickets and two little barks on the lake. With a little exaggeration I could make you believe that nothing ever was so delightful. The idea was really pretty, but as my feelings have lost something of their romantic sensibility, I did not quite enjoy such an entertainment *al fresco* so much as I should have done twenty years ago. The evening was more than cool, and the destined spot anything but dry. There were not half lamps enough, and no music but an ancient militia-man who played cruelly on a squeaking tabor and pipe. As our procession descended the vast flight of steps into the garden, in which was assembled a crowd of people from Buckingham and the neighbouring villages to see the Princess and the show, the moon shining very bright, I could not help laughing, as I surveyed our troop, which instead of tripping lightly to such an Arcadian entertainment, were hobbling down, by the balustrades, wrapped up in cloaks and great-coats for fear of catching cold. The Earl you know is bent double, the Countess very lame, I am a miserable walker, and the Princess though as strong as a Brunswic lion, makes no figure in going down fifty stone stairs. Except Lady Ann – and by courtesy, Lady Mary, we were none of us young enough for a pastoral. We supped in the grotto, which is as proper to this climate, as a sea coal fire would be in the dog-days at Tivoli.

But the chief entertainment of the week, at least what was so to the Princess, is an arch which Lord Temple has erected to her honour in the most enchanting of all picturesque scenes. It is inscribed on one side *Amaeliae Sophiae Aug.* and has a medallion of her on the other. It is placed on an eminence at the top of the Elysian fields, in a grove of orange trees. You come to it on a sudden, and are startled with delight on looking through it: you at once see through a glade the river winding at bottom; from which a thicket rises, arched over with trees, but opened, and discovering a hillock full of haycocks, beyond which in front is the Palladian bridge, and again over that, a larger hill crowned with the castle. It is a tall landscape, framed by the arch and the overbowering trees, and comprehending more beauties of light, shade and buildings, than any picture of Albano I ever saw.

Between the flattery and the prospect the Princess was really in Elysium: she visited her arch four and five times every day, and could not satiate herself with it. The statues of Apollo and the Muses stand on each side of the arch. One day she found in Apollo's hand the following lines, which I had written for her and communicated to Lord Temple;

OVERLEAF
The Elysian Fields, with William Kent's Shell Bridge at the head of the river.

T'other day with a beautiful frown on her brow
To the rest of the gods said the Venus of Stow,
'What a fuss is here made with that arch just erected!
How *our* temples are slighted, our altars neglected!
since yon nymph has appear'd we are – no more
All resort to her shrine, all her presence adore
And what's more provoking, before all our faces
Temple thither has drawn both the Muses and Graces
Keep your temper dear Child, Pheobus cried with a smile
Nor this happy amiable festival spoil
Can your shrine any longer with garlands be drest?
When a true goddess reigns, all the false are supprest.

If you will keep my counsel, I will own to you, that originally the two last lines were much better, but I was forced to alter them out of decorum, not to be too pagan upon the occasion; in short, here they are as in the first sketch.

Recollect, once before that our oracles ceas'd
When a real divinity rose in the East.

So many heathen temples around, had made me talk as a Roman poet would have done; but I corrected my verses, and have made them insipid enough to offend nobody. Good night. I am rejoiced to be once more in the gay solitude of my own little Tempe.

Yours ever
H.W.

Cook's Monument in the Elysian Fields has a portrait of the explorer on the plinth, and is another sign of the imperial vision of the Stowe political circle.

Lady Mary Coke, who was a fellow guest, noted in her journal that Walpole feared a chill from the grotto and 'desired when we came back to the house a glass of cherry brandy by way of prevention'.

Not just the scale of the garden, but the political thinking expressed therein reached a new level under Lord Temple. The vision was now not just national but imperial. The obelisk to Wolfe, who gained Canada for Britain by his brilliant victory at Quebec, has already been mentioned. In the Elysian Fields, a monument was erected in 1778 to Captain Cook, the discoverer, who added Australia to the overseas possessions of His Britannic Majesty. It consisted of a terrestrial globe supported on a square plinth carrying a marble cameo portrait of Cook. Not least, the Grecian Temple was completed in 1762 under Borra's direction, and re-named the Temple of Concord and Victory in celebration of the triumphant ending of the Seven Years' War, which had 'raised Britain from abasement to the first position in the World'. As such it marked the climax of the

The pediment of the Temple of Concord and Victory, depicting Britannia receiving tribute, was carved by Scheemakers and originally adorned the back wall of the Palladian Bridge; it was moved and adapted to its present position in 1762.

Grenville-Pitt policies, for it was due to Pitt's masterly parliamentary leadership that the war, which had begun so badly for Britain with the loss of Minorca and Admiral Byng's unjust court martial for surrendering the island – *'pour encourager les autres'* – was brought to so glorious a conclusion. Both Lord Temple and his younger brother George Grenville, as well as other members of the cousinhood, had all played prominent roles in the wartime cabinet, and could feel well-justified satisfaction in the results. A crowning statue of Victory was added to the topmost pinnacle of the temple and Scheemakers' sculpture of Britannia receiving the tribute of the world (from the Palladian Bridge) was adapted to fit the pediment. Inside, the walls were embellished with stucco Medallions, based on medals designed by James 'Athenian' Stuart, to commemorate the brilliant victories that had given Britain mastery of India and North America. Thus proud, crotchety Lord Temple celebrated 'the triumph of Stowe ideals in a son of Stowe'.

His brother's eldest son George, who succeeded him, and was created Marquess of Buckingham, added the last touches to the garden, though his principal contribution to Stowe was the redecoration and completion of the interior of the house – notably the domed circular saloon behind the south portico – and the enhancement of its collections. For the manuscripts brought from the antiquary Thomas Astle, he commissioned Sir John Soane to design a gothic library in 1805. By 1779, when he inherited, the garden had more or less attained the form in which it survives to this day. Richard Grenville had already introduced Vincenzo Valdrè to his uncle to replace Blondel in about 1776, and he continued to employ him at Stowe in the 1780s, as well as in Ireland while he was Lord-Lieutenant there. Valdrè was almost certainly responsible for the Menagerie (now the school shop), a pretty semi-circular neo-classical building with a domed centre. This was erected in 1781 overlooking an enclosed private flower garden laid out on the site of the old kitchen garden, conveniently close to the south-west corner of the house. He also painted its interior with delightful *trompe l'oeil* trellis murals. Valdrè was also responsible for the last major alteration of one of the Stowe garden buildings, the further remodelling, in 1790, of the former Lady's Temple at the top of Hawkwell Field. It was re-named the Queen's Temple in honour of Queen Charlotte, who had devotedly nursed George III during his serious illness in 1789.* This was not just a disinterested patriotic gesture on Lord Buckingham's part. For if the King had not recovered, a Regency would have had to have been declared, thus opening the way for Fox to become prime minister in place of Buckingham's cousin William Pitt the Younger, who at that stage he staunchly supported. Queen Charlotte had not just nursed the King back to health; she had saved the Pitt-Grenville government!

The old interior with Sleter's murals was replaced with a nobler neo-classical ensemble of stucco and scagliola. The coved ceiling was embellished with plaster ornament inspired by the Temple of the Sun and Moon in Rome. The walls were divided by pilasters in imitation of pink jasper, and ornamented by moulded medallions depicting Britannia weeping for the King's illness, Britannia sacrificing to Aesculapius (god of health) for the King's recovery and the Arts and Sciences flourishing under the King's rule. These were the work of Charles Peart, an Irish artist, and are signed and dated 1790. There was originally a statue of Britannia in the middle of the floor holding a portrait of Queen Charlotte, but this has disappeared.

It was during Lord Buckingham's reign that Stowe became the most famous garden not only in England but in Europe, known and admired as far away as Russia, where the Empress Catherine the Great emulated its layout and buildings at Tsarskoe Selo, like her son and daughter-in-law at Pavlovsk. And Wedgwood's 'Frog Service' for Catherine the Great contains more views of Stowe than any other English scene. In France, too, it was widely admired and written

This plaque in the Queen's Temple shows Britannia sacrificing to Aesculapius, the god of health, for King George III's recovery, and is the work of Charles Peart, an Irish artist. It is dated 1790.

* Valdrè also added the four supporting buttresses, topped by Coade stone lions, to the base of the Cobham Monument at about the same time.

about – by Rousseau among others – and was enthusiastically copied by the anglophile Duc d'Orleans (Philippe Egalité). It became a sort of mecca for English and foreign royalty. Christian VII of Denmark had paid a visit as early as 1768, and of course Frederick, Prince of Wales, and Princess Amelia had graced Stowe with their presence. But under the Marquess of Buckingham the royal visitors became more frequent. The Prince de Condé stayed as his guest in December 1804. Louis XVIII and the French royal family in exile became close friends, and Buckingham found them Hartwell House near Aylesbury as a place of abode. From there they came on a semi-state visit to Stowe in 1809, to commemorate which the former keeper's lodge, an eyecatcher in the eastern part of the park, was enlarged and re-named the 'Bourbon Tower'. George IV came twice as Prince of Wales, in 1805 and 1808. King Gustave of Sweden came in 1810, the Tsar of Russia, Alexander I, in May 1814, the Grand Duke Michael in 1817 and the Grand Duke Nicholas (later Tsar Nicholas I) in 1818. William IV came several times before his accession. And the tradition of royal visits continued well into the nineteenth century. Queen Adelaide was at Stowe in 1840. The King of Hanover came in August 1843, and planted trees in the Orangery Garden at the west end of the house: so did the King of Saxony and the Crown Prince of Prussia.

But not all visitors to Stowe were so exalted. The garden had always been open to the general public. One of Lord Cobham's first buildings had been The New Inn to the south of the grounds (near the site of the Triumphal Arch), for the accommodation of visitors who entered the garden by way of the Bell Gate, next to the east Lake Pavilion. They came in large numbers, and Stowe was one of the first showplaces in England to introduce formal arrangements for tourists with set opening times and official literature. The first guidebook to the garden was published in 1744, twenty years before one was produced for any other comparable garden in England. A guidebook to the Leasowes (a small but much visited garden near Birmingham), for instance, was not printed till 1764, to Lord Lyttelton's garden at Hagley until 1777, and to Blenheim Palace until 1787. The guide published in 1744 by Seeley, an enterprising writing master turned book-seller in Buckingham, was periodically revised and reprinted right up until 1838, when at last it was allowed to go out of print. It is thus a good record of the changing appearance of the garden and buildings from the 1740s to the early nineteenth century.

As well as the guidebook, various other printed works on the garden, some illustrated, were available, including Gilbert West's *Stowe, a Poem* (1732), Rigaud's engravings published by Sarah Bridgeman (1739), William Gilpin's *A Dialogue upon the Gardens at Stow* (1748) and

The Menagerie in the
flower garden, in 1914.
Now the school shop, it
was designed by Valdrè
for the Marquess of
Buckingham and is
among the latest of the
Stowe garden buildings.

George Bickham's *The Beauties of Stowe* (1750), with plans and
engravings. So the visitor to Stowe knew exactly what he was looking
at, and how to respond to the succession of changing historic
landscapes which he was traversing.

In its late eighteenth- and early nineteenth-century prime, Stowe
was visited by curious travellers from all over the world. Many of
them wrote descriptions of what they saw, including Prince Pückler-
Muskau from Poland and Samuel Curwin from America, who visited
in 1777, and began his description thus:

> We arrived at the house, the front of which has a very noble and
> airy appearance. Ascending a lofty flight of steps, we saw an elderly
> person sitting on a settee in half-mourning, by the front door
> under the portico supported by lofty pillars of the Corinthian
> Order. Approaching nearer, I espied a star on his right breast by
> which I recognised the Earl Temple. Pulling off my hat, I was going
> to retire, when he put his hand to his hat and beckoned with the
> other to approach.

The garden as a whole was larger, more varied and more
influential than any other of the age. Its popularity helped to bolster
the political influence of the family, as indeed was the intention. It is
not coincidental that the garden was closed to the public and the
guidebook allowed to fall into dissuetude in the 1830s, after the Great
Reform Bill. George Gilbert Scott, the prolific Victorian architect

OVERLEAF LEFT
The Queen's Temple
from the north.
Originally designed by
James Gibbs for Viscount
Cobham, this elevation
was remodelled for the
Marquess of
Buckingham, probably to
the design of Vincenzo
Valdrè, one of a number
of foreign architects
employed in the final
phases of the Stowe
landscape.

RIGHT
The Bourbon Tower, an
eyecatcher outside the
garden to the east, was
built as a keeper's lodge
to Vanbrugh's design. It
was remodelled and re-
named to commemorate
Louis XVIII's visit to
Stowe in 1808, when the
French royal family was
in exile at nearby
Hartwell.

Jacques Rigaud's views of 1739 from the south-west bastion of the ha-ha across the Eleven-Acre Lake, and south from the house over the parterre and down the Abele Walk.

who was brought up in Buckinghamshire not far from Stowe, remembered the estate as an aloof and inaccessible place, guarded by gamekeepers, but then as a Goth he would have been prejudiced against its classical architecture and 'cold unfeeling portico'. His response was ironic, for Stowe was created as an expression of the 'ideals of liberty and natural order fundamental to the human condition', a living symbol of the curbing of tyranny.

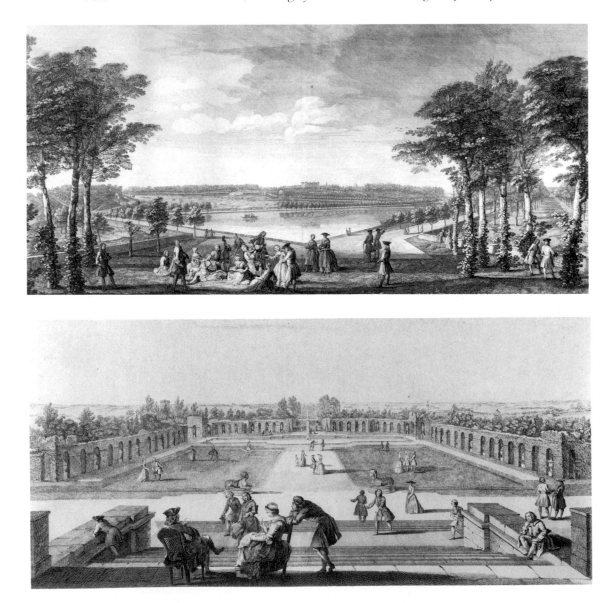

V

DECLINE AND FALL

Stowe has 'thrown open its portals to an endless succession of visitors who from morning to night have flowed in an uninterrupted stream from room to room and floor to floor — not to enjoy the hospitality of the Lord, or to congratulate him on his countless treasures of art, but to see an ancient family ruined, their palace marked for destruction, and its contents scattered to the four winds of Heaven ... the Duke of Buckingham and Chandos, is at the moment an absolutely ruined and destitute man ... Stowe is no more ....

Neither Louis XVIII, nor the Duke of Orleans, nor Queen Victoria, not any of the great ones of the earth, whose visits are recorded with pillars and with trees, saw Stowe so nobly arrayed as the British public have seen it this week. The Bride was dressed for the altar, the victim for the sacrifice ... King Mob had it all of the best ....

These columns have spared neither people nor prince .... Should we deal fairly if we spared the destroyer of his house, the man whose reckless course has thrown to the ground a pillar of the state, and struck a heavy blow to the order to which he unfortunately belongs? .... The Duke of Buckingham has filled all minds with the painful presage of a wider ruin. Such events speak in these days. When dynasties are falling and aristocracies have crumbled into dust, disgrace acquires the force of injury, and personal ruin is a public treason. ... [The Duke] has reduced his honours to the tinsel of a pauper and the baubles of a fool.'

LORD MACAULAY, *editorial in* The Times, *14 August 1848*

O N THE DEATH OF THE Marquess of Buckingham in 1813, he was succeeded by his son Richard Temple-Nugent-Brydges-Chandos-Grenville, who fulfilled the hereditary family ambition and was created Duke of Buckingham and Chandos in 1824. In his reign little was changed in the gardens; he concentrated mainly on the collections inside the house, adding a museum of natural curiosities and an outstanding assemblage of prints and engravings to the Old Master paintings, antique sculpture, English and Continental furniture, books and manuscripts assembled by his predecessors, as well as the large inheritance of his wife Lady Anna Eliza Brydges, Baroness Kinloss. He adhered to family tradition by going into politics and served as joint Paymaster-General and Deputy-President of the Board of Trade in the family government of 1806–7, when his uncle Lord Grenville was prime minister. During the 'Hundred Days' after Napoleon had escaped from Elba and once more assembled an army in France to fight the allies, he took a regiment of the Buckinghamshire Militia across the Channel to Flanders and served in the British army under Wellington.

But the great days of Stowe were nearly over. Already in 1804 under the Marquess of Buckingham, the painter and diarist William Farington had reported that although the estate income was large,* it took a year and a half or two years for accounts to be settled. With the death of the Marquess of Buckingham in 1813, the family's immense sinecure revenue from the government, including the lucrative Tellership of the Exchequer, ceased. Building and planting on the scale of Stowe would have stretched any private family's resources. And on top of that there was the enormous cost of the Grenvilles' political role, with all the election 'expenses' which were essential under the unreformed parliamentary franchise if the voters were complaisantly to return a Pitt, a Grenville or a Lyttelton, as required, to the House of Commons. Partly with the aim of extending the family's parliamentary influence and also out of pure self-aggrandisement, large sums of money had been borrowed to enlarge the estate till it covered over 50,000 acres. By the 1st Duke's time this fatal policy had lumbered future generations with a mortgage and running debt of over a million pounds, in those days an enormous sum of money. It was his worsening financial situation which forced him to close Stowe in 1827 and go abroad for three years. But his travels were conducted on such a scale that it is doubtful whether they turned out to be much of an economy measure. He

* In the early nineteenth century the estate income was c.£64,000 a year.

cruised around the Mediterranean on a large private yacht named after his wife the *Anna Eliza*, and continued to collect geological specimens, as well as financing various archaeological excavations. While in Rome in 1828 he bought a large antique marble sarcophagus which became his prize possession. On his return home, he erected it in the garden at Stowe as a tomb for his favourite dog, a red-nosed pug called Harlequin.

He died in 1839 and was succeeded as 2nd Duke by his son, also Richard, who married Lady Mary Campbell, daughter of the 1st Marquess of Breadalbane. The 2nd Duke had sat in the House of Commons till he was translated to the Lords in 1839 and is best known as the proposer of the Chandos Clause in the Great Reform Bill of 1832, which extended the franchise in counties to £50 tenants at will in addition to freehold owners and leaseholders. He was a great upholder of the agricultural interest and opponent of the Corn Laws. He broke with the Prime Minister, Sir Robert Peel, when the latter introduced a sliding scale of duties on corn which he saw, rightly, as the 'thin end of the wedge'. He resigned as a result, marking the end of the long tradition of Grenville service in the government. He has the unusual, if dubious distinction of having

J. C. Buckler's view of the north front in 1815, showing the flanking colonnades added by Lord Temple, and the portico attributed to Vanbrugh.

been caricatured in several political novels, as the 'Marquess of Vipont' in Edward Bulwer-Lytton's *What Will He Do With It?*, for instance, and as the Duke of Agincourt in Disraeli's *Coningsby*.

He failed totally to tackle the financial problems facing Stowe. Indeed by reckless expenditure and gross mismanagement he exacerbated the situation, and within eight years had brought down ruin on himself and his family. He had one last fling, however. In 1844 he managed to invite Queen Victoria and Prince Albert to Stowe for a spectacular visit. In the 1840s, in the years after her marriage, the Queen (with Prince Albert) made a point of staying with her subjects in their country seats. But by what seemed to the Grenvilles an unimaginable oversight, Stowe had not been included in the first list of chosen houses. Whatever else he may have lacked, the duke suffered from no underestimation of his own consequence, and immediately made known his feelings to Sir Robert Peel. The latter was able to arrange that the royal train, *en route* for Chatsworth, would stop for twenty-four hours at Wolverton so that the Queen could take in Stowe. This was not good enough for the duke. He wrote to Peel: 'We did hope that the *same* period which Her Majesty had honoured *other* individuals would have been allowed to us . . . I assure you I feel it very much indeed.' This second pained protest caused the visit to be extended for a further day, so that the royal couple could spend the night under the ducal roof. 'The Duke behaved as only a genuine Regency rake in debt up to his ears could have done. The entire Regiment of Yeomanry was called out; nearly

Queen Victoria's visit to Stowe in 1846 was Stowe's swansong. Two years later the Duke of Buckingham was bankrupt, and the contents of the house were dispersed by Christie's in a sale which lasted for forty days.

a thousand tenants and labourers lined the approaches to Stowe; three orchestras and a squad of police were brought from London; and several rooms were refurnished for the royal visitors.'

Legend has it that when Queen Victoria and Prince Albert strolled round the gardens, now in their full maturity with many of the trees over a century old, the chorus from Covent Garden had been placed at strategic intervals and 'sang like nightingales' as the royal couple passed by. Whatever the exact details of the entertainment provided, there is little doubt that this piece of ducal extravagance was the final straw. The duke's request to his eldest son in 1847 to agree, as the heir, to an additional capital sum of £350,000 being raised from the entailed estates, over and above the existing mortgage of £1,100,000, led to a flat refusal. Lord Chandos, the son, came up with a counter-proposal for the family trustees to implement. This was that the duke should hand over his life-interest in the whole property in return for an agreed annual income, and that the son would assume responsibility for the debts; he would attempt to sort out the family finances as best he could. After some blustering the duke agreed, but the principal creditors insisted on the contents of the house being sold to meet the immediate sums outstanding. And so Christie and Manson (as the firm was then called) were summoned to auction the Grenville chattels, 'amounting in total to 5,000 lots, including 1,750 dozen of wine and 60,000 ounces of silver'.

The auction itself was held in the state dining-room and began on 15 August 1848, lasting for forty days (a good biblical number to rub in the moral to an appreciative Victorian audience). The post-sale catalogue began with the customary regrets: 'There are few spectacles more saddening to a generous mind than the decadence from its "palmy estate" of so noble and time-honoured a family as that of Buckingham and Chandos ...'. One can almost hear the auctioneers rubbing their hands and totting up their commission! Though the auction was restricted mainly to the contents of the house, some of the garden sculpture was sold as well, including the 1st Duke's prized Roman sarcophagus – presumably Harlequin was decently re-interred in a nearby flowerbed. The movable furniture from the temples (including the busts from the Temple of Friendship) was also dispersed. The grand total realized by the sale came to £75,562 4s 6d – less than was anticipated. The duke himself disappeared to lodging in Wilton Place, 'where he occupied himself with his Memoirs and the wife of a clerk to the House of Lords. He died in 1861 amid the bourgeois opulence of the Great Western Hotel, Paddington.'

In the event, the 3rd Duke was able to save quite a lot from the wreckage, including the house, the gardens, and the nucleus of the estate, and either to buy in or otherwise acquire suitable furnishings for the main rooms, so that, though not what it had been before 1848, Stowe still presented a very favourable appearance to the world. Some 40,000 acres of land were sold to pay off the mortgage, but the duke kept 10,000 acres immediately around Stowe itself. He continued to maintain the gardens properly, and made a special point at the Stowe sale of buying in some of the decorative statuary, such as Laurent Delvaux's group of Vertumnus and Pomona from the south portico. This piece of sculpture had come with the Chandos heirlooms and was probably made originally for the garden at Canons, Middlesex, the short-lived Chandos seat for the chapel at which Handel had composed the Chandos Anthems. In some ways the collapse of the family finances was a blessing, for it prevented any further alterations or developments in the garden and enabled the eighteenth-century layout to survive into the twentieth century largely in the form in which it was left in 1780, with no Victorian alterations at all.

The interior of the Palladian Bridge. The ceiling based on an antique original at Palmyra was installed by Borra in the 1760s.

The 3rd Duke finally broke with the Whig tradition of his family and became a Conservative, as had been presaged by his predecessor's political deals with Liverpool and Peel. He was MP for Buckingham from 1846 till 1857, and one of the Lords of the Treasury in 1852. He was the model of the public-spirited Victorian aristocrat, just as his father had been an archetypal Regency rake. He was Privy Seal to the Prince of Wales (later Edward VII), Secretary of State for the Colonies, Lord-Lieutenant of Buckinghamshire and, finally, Governor of Madras from 1875 to 1880. His career added up to a respectable twilight for Stowe. Though he married twice, the 3rd Duke produced no son, and on his death in 1889 the dukedom became extinct. But because of a series of special remainders in the patents of creation, some of the other titles were inherited through the female line by a varied assortment of heirs, and have thus survived to the present day. The earldom of Temple of Stowe was inherited by a Gore-Langton nephew (his mother was the duke's sister). The viscounty of Cobham passed to cousins, the Lytteltons of Hagley, while the 3rd Duke's eldest daughter inherited the barony of Kinloss, a Scottish title which could pass through the female line and had come into the family as part of the Chandos inheritance.

Baroness Kinloss had no use for so vast a house and let it. Thus Stowe entered into the first, but not the least improbable, of its after-lives, as a palace-in-exile for the pretender to the French throne, Louis-Philippe Albert, Comte de Paris, head of the Orleans branch of the royal House of Bourbon. The Comte de Paris leased the house in

1889 because it reminded him, so he said, of Versailles, presumably an allusion to the scale rather than the style. He took up residence the following year with his wife and five younger children; the eldest daughter was Queen of Portugal, and the eldest son, the Duc d'Orleans, spent most of his time travelling restlessly abroad. The Comte de Paris was the grandson and heir of King Louis-Philippe and had spent much of his earlier life in England after his grandfather's abdication in 1848. The French royal family, having returned to live as private citizens in Paris in 1871, had been expelled from France for a second time in 1886 and so were already looking for a suitable place of residence in England when Stowe became available. It was appropriate in many ways, not least because there was in any case a long history of friendship between the French royal family and the Grenvilles, going back to the Duc d'Orlean's visits to England in the late eighteenth century and Louis XVIII's exile in Buckinghamshire.

The French family seem to have been popular at Stowe, the countess in particular, for she rode to hounds and smoked cigars. Notices in French were put up at Buckingham railway station for the convenience of their guests. The Comte de Paris died at Stowe in 1894 and lay in state in the Marble Saloon. The Prince of Wales visited Stowe to present his condolences to the 25-year-old heir, the Duc d'Orleans, and a surviving photograph shows them, top-hatted, on the steps leading to the north portico. As tenants, the Orleans made few alterations to the gardens, but they did add another to Stowe's miscellaneous collection of dogs' graves. A weathered headstone under a tulip tree near the south front reads 'For twelve years a faithful and devoted companion of the Comte de Paris'; the name is illegible.

Two years after the Comte's death his family moved back to Twickenham (where Louis-Philippe had lived in exile), and Stowe slumbered once more under dust sheets. Slowly the temples, pavilions and shrines began to crumble. Evocative photographs taken by *Country Life* at the turn of the century show the grounds still kept up, but many traces of picturesque decay – bits of cornice falling off some of the buildings, and paterae or dentils missing from the friezes. To the Baroness Kinloss Stowe appeared, no doubt, as a huge 'white elephant'. Her eldest son, the Master of Kinloss, was killed in action in December 1914, and though his three brothers survived World War I, the death of the heir in his twenties must have contributed to the decision to give up Stowe. The final sale was held in July 1921 and lasted for eighteen days. It was conducted by the local firm of Jackson-Stops and Staff and made their fortune. The contents of the house, including those items retained by the family in 1848 and

The Fane of Pastoral Poetry was originally designed by James Gibbs in the west garden, but was moved to the north-east corner of the ha-ha by Lord Temple as part of his remodelling and thinning programme in the 1760s.

the nineteenth-century accretions, were all disposed of. But, in the hope of saving it, the house and grounds were offered as a single lot. Fortunately, Stowe had survived into an age when a handful of pioneer Georgian enthusiasts appreciated it as a magnificent example of Georgian art. There was widespread public interest and articles in the press. The editor of *The Spectator*, for instance, published a piece about the place, its past, its present state, and its possible future written by his son-in-law, the architect Clough Williams-Ellis, which was to have an unforeseen and rather amusing consequence.

The house and grounds were bought *en bloc* at the auction by Mr

This urn in the Elysian Fields, photographed in 1914, was among the garden ornaments lost in the sale in 1921.

Harry Shaw, a property developer. But he had difficulty in raising the necessary money and therefore instructed Jackson-Stops to resell the place. It was at this stage that many of the statues, urns and small decorative items from the grounds, including the Greek heroes from the Temple of Ancient Virtue, Mercury from the British Worthies, Apollo and the Muses, the Pomona, and the lions from the south portico, the herms from the north front and the Menagerie, and five of the crowning statues from Concord and Victory were sold. Even the bronze urns from the balustrade in front of the house were removed and sold. None of these things should have left Stowe, as they were an integral part of the original architecture. Today it would not have been possible to remove them, for Stowe is a Grade I listed building. But historic buildings in England have had legal protection only since World War II and in 1921 there were no regulations or laws to prevent Stowe from being mutilated or demolished. It could easily have gone the way of so many other fine houses in the 1920s and been totally destroyed. That it did not do so was thanks to the intervention of a dedicated group of private individuals.

The south front of the house at the beginning of this century. The statuary in the portico, the lions flanking the staircase and the bronze urns were all sold in 1921.

AFTERMATH

AT THE END of World War I there was a shortage of places at the major public schools. No new ones had been founded for more than sixty years, during which time the population and national wealth had expanded considerably. A movement was set in train to create a large new school 'to be both traditional and adventurous and to rank, if possible, among the first six'. When Stowe was put up for sale in 1921, the school's promoters saw it as providing an incomparable setting for the new establishment they had in mind. When the house and gardens were acquired as one lot by Mr Harry Shaw, he offered them for the use of the new school then under consideration, provided that an endowment fund could be established. A committee was formed for this purpose but failed.

When he instructed the house to be resold it looked as if Stowe was doomed to be broken up. But a second and stronger committee was set up within ten days of the first auction and it saved the situation. Stowe School was born on 11 May 1923 under a headmaster of genius, J. F. Roxburgh, previously the second Master at Lancing in Sussex. Thus the great landscape setting was rescued to serve, 'in the way that is perhaps the most appropriate under today's conditions the humanist ideals underlying its creation' (Christopher Hussey). It was a brave and imaginative undertaking to take on Stowe, but worthwhile, for the landscape and architecture have had a profound effect on the developing character of the school. This was the founders' intention. For, as Roxburgh himself said, 'If we do not fail in our purpose, every boy who goes out from Stowe will know beauty when he sees it for the rest of his life.'

The place needed a considerable degree of repair and adaptation before the school could open. Clough Williams-Ellis was chosen as the architect on the strength of his piece in *The Spectator*. The story is best told in his own words: 'It was a week or two after my article had appeared that a Mr. Percy Warrington was announced at my office as wishing to see me "about Stowe". There entered a short, tubby, clerical figure rather reminiscent of Chesterton's Father Brown, but entirely lacking his touching humility; on the contrary indeed, exuding self-importance and bustling enterprise. He had been much interested, he said, in my account of Stowe and my suggestions for its future use, but that had in fact already been settled as he had arranged to acquire it as the latest link in a chain of schools that he himself was in the process of establishing. Would I care to help the project with ideas, if not with publicity or money?

I explained that I was not a columnist nor a fund-raiser, but an architect, but that *as* such I should of course be proud to follow where my illustrious predecessors had so brilliantly left their mark — Vanbrugh, Gibbs, Robert Adam, Bridgeman, Capability Brown, Soane and the rest — if his colleagues so decided. It then appeared that

The Pebble Alcove, with a pebble mosaic depicting Lord Cobham's coat of arms, is one of the buildings restored in recent years by Stowe School.

The portico of the Temple of Friendship, showing the decayed condition of the fabric.

he was already assembling a Board of Governors for his projected new public school which, though including a Bishop, a General and a couple of peers, would, he assured me, certainly accept his decision as to the appointment of an architect as in most matters. After all the whole financing of the project depended entirely on him alone.'

So Clough found himself with the job and was soon inspecting the long-neglected house. Counting the rooms on a survey plan he found that there were four hundred. But there was not much of anything else: no water supply, no drains, no heating, no lighting. Somehow the huge, inadequately maintained building had to be transformed into a reasonably functioning school for two hundred boys in four separate 'houses'; the numbers to be increased threefold later on. It was a knotty problem to provide both the necessary accommodation and all the services without disturbing the historic fabric too drastically, as well as carrying out the work within the tight deadline allowed.

But no sooner had this transformation been put in hand than a number of additional new buildings were requested by the school governors, including two classroom blocks, laboratories, a sanatorium, a gym, squash courts and a completely new boarding house. It is a great pity that a proper master-plan was not devised for these, and any future expansion, but such was the tightness of the schedule, and the piecemeal nature of the building programme — dependent on the funds raised at any one time — that it is understandable that things were rushed into at the beginning without due foresight. It was, however, agreed that the main vistas were to be sacrosanct, but it was hoped, optimistically, that additional buildings could be tacked on at the east and west ends of the house without being too obtrusive. And in some instances this proved right. Clough's westwards extension of the Orangery to create a symmetrical garden court, for instance, is remarkably tactful. But as the new buildings spread outwards they became more and more visible, and the whole of Nelson's Walk to the west was eventually to be engulfed by miscellaneous structures which harmonized ill with masterpieces by Gibbs, Kent and Vanbrugh. Even Clough's own new house, Chatham House, is in full view of Kent's Temple of Venus and Vanbrugh's Rotunda and is built of bright red brick, hardly a sympathetic material at Stowe.

Clough's heart, though, was in the right place. He was sad to see all the statuary go in the second sale (apart from George I, Queen Caroline and the British Worthies), and he did his best to encourage the school to make good the depredations. He was personally responsible for restoring a pair of sculpted lions to the plinths flanking the great flight of steps to the south portico. (The originals now ornament the roof balustrade of Easton Neston in Northamptonshire, having been bought by Lord Hesketh at the 1921 sale.) Clough's own description is inimitable. 'Somehow I contrived to get plausible understudies to occupy the plinths of those noble lions, cast in concrete from models made for me by the sculptor John Bickerdyke — less noble, even 'Utility Lions' — but still preserving the general feeling of the grand approach.' He himself bought Rysbrack's marble Friga as a memento; she had been left behind after the sale having for superstitious reasons failed to find a buyer. The other six Saxon deities had been sold as individual lots. 'When some long time after buying her I had chosen her intended site and wanted to bring her away, search as I might I entirely failed to find her . . . So I offered a reward to the first schoolboy to discover her hiding place and we

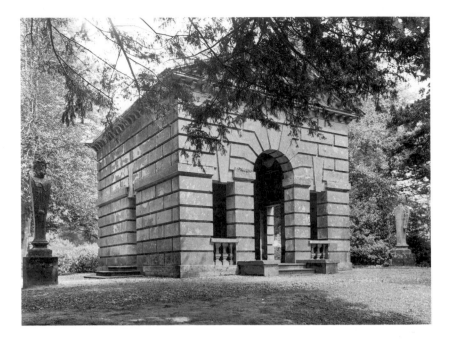

Vanbrugh's Temple of
Bacchus in 1914.
Demolished to make way
for the school chapel,
this was the only
important loss among
the Stowe garden
buildings.

were soon re-united.' She is now at Portmeirion, Clough's Italianate
holiday village in North Wales.

The aspect of the sales which most distressed Clough was the
school governors' decision not to bid for the Grand Avenue. It was
offered for sale in seven lots as sites for a ribbon development of villas
or bungalows. Clough pointed out that this would not only be the
destruction of the finest avenue in England but would ruin the new
school's main approach. But the Governors said they could not
afford to buy another square yard. So Clough attended the auction
and bought the whole thing himself, in order to preserve the avenue
intact. He was not able to hold it indefinitely, however, so he put an
advertisement in *The Times*. This brought an immediate response
from the Vice-Provost of Eton, who thought it would be an
appropriate gesture if Old Etonians presented the avenue 'as a sort of
christening present' to the new school. The presentation was made
at a ceremonial occasion with Prince Arthur of Connaught, Queen
Victoria's son, unlocking symbolical gates that Clough designed to
go between Valdrè's lodges at the Buckingham entrance. A plaque
on one of the lodges, in beautifully phrased Latin by the Vice-
Provost, now marks the gift: '1924. That the voice of their murmuring
leaves might not be silenced, Etonians redeemed these trees and
offered them to the new-born school with this prayer: that it stand
fast and stand first. July 17th.'

OVERLEAF
The principal approach
to Stowe is the Grand
Avenue, which runs 2½
miles from Buckingham;
the spire of the town's
parish church is a
conspicuous feature in
the view south. The
original planting of elms
has had to be replaced
and the avenue is now
composed of alternate
blocks of beech and
chestnut.

LEFT
The school chapel
designed by Sir Robert
Lorimer, the
distinguished Scottish
architect who died in
1929. It was one of the first
buildings added to Stowe
after it became a public
school.

After Clough, the school employed Fielding Dodd to design
further extensions in the 1930s. He was responsible for Walpole House
and court at the east end of the house which happily perpetuates the
style of the old outbuildings. He was also the author of the neo-
Georgian cricket pavilion on the north lawn. The finest of the new
school buildings is the basilican chapel designed by Sir Robert
Lorimer, though it is regrettable, to say the least, that Vanbrugh's
Temple of Bacchus was demolished to make way for it, and that
sixteen fluted columns were removed from the back and sides of the
Temple of Concord and Victory to adorn its interior. Of the many
post-war school buildings, none is architecturally worthy of Stowe
and some are atrociously sited.

But if it were not for the school there would be nothing left of the

garden and its temples. In 1921 house and grounds were threatened by the house-breakers, and much of the eighteenth-century architecture was in a somewhat decayed condition. Serious plans were drawn up in the 1930s to repair each of the buildings in turn, but only the Queen's Temple was tackled before World War II intervened. The programme was revived in the 1950s with generous assistance from the Historic Buildings Council, but funds were always in short supply. In 1965 the architect Hugh Creighton produced a report on all the buildings as the basis for a continuing programme and a separate Garden Building Trust was later established to raise funds; 26 structures have been tackled on this basis, including the Pebble Alcove, the Temple of Ancient Virtue, the Cobham Monument, the ha-ha and the cascades. The boys themselves helped with forestry work, clearing undergrowth and thinning plantations, as well as dredging the various lakes and pools. But much still remained to be done. In 1967 the school governors entered into covenants with the National Trust to ensure the preservation of all the landscape gardens south and east of the house; the National Trust acquired the Oxford Avenue separately, in 1984, from the great-great-grandson of the last duke. It was therefore the logical conclusion when the school transferred the majority of the historic landscape layout to the Trust in 1989. A ten-year restoration programme has now been embarked on by the Trust, and a major appeal launched to raise the necessary funds, so that this greatest of eighteenth-century landscape gardens can be preserved for the future.

The generosity of an anonymous benefactor — together with a very large additional sum from the National Heritage Memorial Fund — has made this longer-term solution possible, which will enable the gardens to be adequately endowed and maintained.

Substantial funds still need to be raised to repair individual buildings, such as Kent's Temple of Venus in the south-west bastion of the ha-ha, or the Temple of Concord and Victory with its giant Ionic columns. But in the words of Gervase Jackson-Stops of the National Trust: 'The partnership between Stowe School and the National Trust, and the wealth of documentation that exists to guide the work of the restorers, makes this one of the most exciting projects of its kind ever undertaken. In time there is no doubt that Stowe will once more take its place as a garden of international importance, comparable with masterpieces such as Vaux-le-Vicomte or the Villa Lante. Historians will continue to argue about its evolution, and make discoveries about its different components, but in the end its haunting beauty, defying rational analysis, and as complex as the English character itself, will triumph.'

APPENDIX

*Edward Bulwer-Lytton's Caricature of the
Temple-Grenvilles of Stowe as the Viponts in
What Will He Do With It?*

THE HOUSE OF VIPONT! Looking back through ages, it seems as if the House of Vipont were one continuous living idiosyncrasy, having in its progressive development a connected unity of thought and action, so that through all the changes of its outward form it had been moved and guided by the same single spirit – 'Le roi est mort – vive le roi!' – A Vipont dies – live the Vipont!

* * *

It was not, however, till the Government, under Sir Robert Walpole, established the constitutional and parliamentary system which characterizes modern freedom, that the puissance accumulated through successive centuries by the House of Vipont became pre-eminently visible. By that time its lands were vast, its wealth enormous; its parliamentary influence, as 'a Great House,' was a part of the British Constitution. At this period, the House of Vipont found it convenient to rend itself into two grand divisions – the peer's branch and the commoner's. The House of Commons had become so important that it was necessary for the House of Vipont to be represented there by a great commoner. Thus arose the family of Carr Vipont. That division, owing to a marriage settlement favouring a younger son by the heiress of the Carrs, carried off a good slice from the estate of the earldom; – uno adverso, non deficit alter, – the earldom mourned, but replaced the loss by two wealthy wedlocks of its own; and had long since seen cause to rejoice that its power in the Upper Chamber was strengthened by such aid in the Lower. For, thanks to its parliamentary influence, and the aid of the great commoner, in the reign of George III the House of Vipont became a Marquess. From that time to the present day, the House of Vipont had gone on prospering and progressive. It was to the aristocracy what the Times newspaper is to the press. The same quick sympathy with public feeling – the same unity of tone and purpose – the same adaptability – and something of the same lofty tone of superiority to the petty interests of party. It may be conceded that the House of Vipont was less brilliant than the Times newspaper, but eloquence and wit, necessary to the duration of a newspaper, were not necessary to that of the House of Vipont. Had they been so, it would have had them.

The head of the House of Vipont rarely condescended to take office. With a rent-roll loosely estimated at about £170,000 a-year, it is beneath a man to take from the public a paltry five or six thousand a-year, and undergo all the undignified abuse of popular assemblies, and 'a ribald press'. But it was a matter of course that the House of Vipont should be represented in any cabinet that a constitutional monarch could be advised to form. Since the time of Walpole, a Vipont was always in the service of his country, except in those rare instances when the country was infamously misgoverned. The cadets of the House, or the senior member of the great commoner's branch of it, sacrificed their ease to fulfil that duty. The Montfort marquesses in general were contented with situations of honour in the household, as of Lord Steward, Lord Chamberlain, or Master of the Horse, &c. – not onerous dignities; and even these they only deigned to accept on those special occasions when danger threatened the Star of Brunswick, and the sense of its exalted station forbade the House of Vipont to leave its country in the dark.

Great Houses like that of Vipont assist the work of civilization by the law of their existence. They are sure to have a spirited and wealthy tenantry, to whom, if but for the sake of that popular character which doubles political influence, they are liberal and kindly landlords. Under their sway fens and sands become fertile — agricultural experiments are tested on a large scale — cattle and sheep improve in breed — national capital augments, and springing beneath the ploughshare, circulates indirectly to speed the ship and animate the loom. Had there been no Woburn, no Holkham, no Montfort Court, England would be the poorer by many a million. Our Great Houses tend also to the refinement of national taste; they have their show places, their picture galleries, their beautiful grounds. The humblest drawing-rooms owe an elegance or comfort — the smallest garden a flower or esculent — to the importations which luxury borrowed from abroad, or the inventions it stimulated at home, for the original benefit of Great Houses. Having a fair share of such merits, in common with other Great Houses, the House of Vipont was not without good qualities peculiar to itself. Precisely because it was the most egotistical of Houses, filled with the sense of its own identity, and guided by the instincts of its own conservation, it was a very civil, good-natured House — courteous, generous, hospitable; a House (I mean the head of it, not of course all its subordinate members, including even the august Lady Selina) that could bow graciously and shake hands with you. Even if you had no vote yourself, you might have a cousin who had a vote. And once admitted into the family, the House adopted you; you had only to marry one of its remotest relations, and the House sent you a wedding present; and at every general election, invited you to rally round your connection — the Marquess. Therefore, next only to the Established Church, the House of Vipont was that British insitution the roots of which were the most widely spread.

FURTHER READING

ORIGINAL SOURCES

The Stowe family papers

An immense collection of over half a million items left the house at the final sale in 1921 and is now in the Henry E. Huntington Library, San Marino, California.

A small part of this collection by chance escaped the auctioneer's hammer and is still in the School Library, including photographs of Stowe in the occupation of the Comte de Paris.

The Stowe guidebooks

Mainly published by Seeley, bookseller, of Buckingham. These begin in 1744 and run on till 1838, constantly revised. In them the development of Stowe can be followed in much detail. Engraved illustrations, and sometimes maps, appear in many of the guides. These were sold separately, to be bound up with the guide if the purchaser so wished. They are consequently often out of date for the copy in which they appear. Among guides may be included *A Dialogue upon the Gardens at Stow*, 1748 (published anonymously, but by William Gilpin); and *The Beauties of Stowe* (with map and illustrations) by George Bickham, 1750. (The School Library has the best collection in existence of Stowe guides.)

Miscellaneous illustrations

A low-oblique aerial view of Stowe from the south-west. Original drawing by Charles Bridgeman, *c*.1719. Bodleian Library (MS Gough Drawings, a. 4. Fol. 46).

A specially bound and grangerized elephant-folio copy of Daniel Lysons' *Magna Britannia*, Volume 1, Part 2 (Buckinghamshire), originally made up in 1820 for William, Lord Grenville (now the property of Gerard Morgan-Grenville.)

Drawings of Stowe by John Claude Nattes 1805–9 in the Buckinghamshire County Museum (published by Buckinghamshire County Museum and Stowe School, 1983).

Eighteenth-century publications

Gibbs, James, *A Book of Architecture* (1728).

Pope, Alexander, *Of Taste: An Epistle to the Earl of Burlington* (1731).

West, Gilbert, *Stowe* (1732) a descriptive poem by Lord Cobham's nephew.

The Triumph of Nature, an anonymous poem descriptive of Stowe, printed in *The Gentleman's Magazine* (1742).

Appendix to *A Tour through Britain, by a Gentleman*, Vol. III, p. 271, anon, 1742.

Fifteen views of Stowe drawn by Jacques Rigaud, *c*.1733, and engraved by himself and Bernard Baron. Issued by Sarah Bridgeman (the garden-designer's widow) in 1739, with a map of that date. Published for binding up, with a title-page, by Thomas Bowles, 1746.

Sixteen views of Stowe drawn by J.-B. Chatelain in 1752 and engraved with a map, by George Bickham, 1753.

Modern reprints

Clarke, George B., ed., *Descriptions of Lord Cobham's Garden at Stowe* (Buckinghamshire Record Society, 1990).

Dixon Hunt, John, ed., 'The Gardens of Stowe', *The English Garden*, XVI (1982).

Weinreb, Ben, *Bridgeman's Stowe*, a facsimile of the 1739 edition issued by Sarah Bridgeman (see above), with notes on each of the views and an afterword by George B. Clarke (1987).

SECONDARY WORKS

Apollo, June 1973 (whole issue devoted to Stowe).

Annan, Lord, *Roxburgh of Stowe* (1965).

Buckingham & Chandos, 2nd Duke of, *Memoirs of the Court and Cabinets of George III*, 2 vols (1853).

Country Life (25 articles, 1905–1989).

Croom-Johnson, R. P., *The Origin of Stowe School* (1953).

Dixon Hunt, John, 'Emblem and Expression in the 18th century Landscape Garden', *Eighteenth Century Studies* IV (1971), 294–317.

Friedman, Terry, *James Gibbs* (1985).

Harris, John, 'Blondel at Stowe', *Connoisseur* (March 1964).

Hussey, Christopher, *English Gardens and Landscapes 1700–1750* (1967).

McCarthy, Michael, 'Eighteenth-Century Amateur Architects and Their Gardens', in N. Pevsner, ed., *The Picturesque Garden*, (1974), 31–55.

McCarthy, Michael, 'James Lovell and His Sculptures at Stowe', *Burlington Magazine* (April 1973).

Macdonald, Alasdair, *Stowe House and School* (1951).

Ramsey Forster, Henry, *Stowe Catalogue* (1848).

Rosebery, 3rd Earl of, *Chatham, His Early Life and Connections* (1910).

Smith, N. J. *The Grenville Correspondence*, 3 vols (1852).

The Stoic, April 1933, December 1950, August 1965, March 1967–December 1977, I–XXVI (Articles by George Clarke and Michael Gibbon on the history and development of the gardens at Stowe).

Speak, W. A., 'Political Propaganda in Augustan England', *Royal Historical Society Transactions*, Series 5, XXII (1972).

Stroud, Dorothy, *Capability Brown* (1950, 3rd edition, 1975).

Whistler, Lawrence, *The Imagination of Vanbrugh and His Fellow Artists* (1954).

Whistler, Lawrence, Gibbon, Michael, and Clarke, George, *Stowe: A Guide to the Gardens* (1956, 3rd edition, 1974).

Wiggin, Lewis, *Faction of Cousins: A Political Account of the Grenvilles 1733–63* (1958).

Williams-Ellis, Clough, *Architect Errant* (1971).

Willis, Peter, *Charles Bridgeman* (1977).

Willis, Peter, 'Jacques Rigaud's Drawings of Stowe in the Metropolitan Museum of Art', *Eighteenth Century Studies* VI (1972), 85–98.

INDEX

ILLUSTRATION SOURCES AND ACKNOWLEDGMENTS

Ashmolean Museum, Oxford p. 99; The Bodleian Library, Oxford pp. 68–9; courtesy of *Country Life* pp. 116, 120–21, 130, 147, 166–7; Metropolitan Museum of Art, New York p. 30; courtesy of Gerard Morgan-Grenville Esq. p. 151; courtesy of John Morgan-Grenville Esq. p. 152; National Portrait Gallery pp. 35, 63, 77, 82, 102; The National Trust Photographic Library/Jerry Harpur pp. 21, 23, 47, 90, 119, 124, 125, 135, 143, 162, 165; courtesy of the Trustees of Sir John Soane's Museum pp. 126–7; Stowe School pp. 11, 30, 34, 42, 53, 54, 64, 65, 74, 76, 77 (right), 85, 86, 109, 136, 148; Vergnaud, *L'Art de Créer les Jardins* (Paris, 1835; trans. L. Archer-Hind, ed. W. C. Wright as *A History of Garden Art*, 1928) pp. 13, 118; by courtesy of the Wedgwood Museum Trustees p. 14.